BARRON'S

IELTS®

STRATEGIES AND TIPS

BARRON'S

IELTS®

STRATEGIES AND TIPS

Lin Lougheed, Ed.D.
Teachers College
Columbia University

All inquiries should be addressed to:
Barron's Educational Series, Inc.
250 Wireless Boulevard
Hauppauge, New York 11788
www.barronseduc.com

Library of Congress Catalog No.: 2013943166

ISBN: 978-1-4380-7365-1

PRINTED IN THE UNITED STATES OF AMERICA
9 8 7 6 5 4

CONTENTS

INTRODUCTION

IELTS LISTENING MODULE

IELTS READING MODULE

IELTS SPEAKING MODULE

APPENDIX

INTRODUCTION

Definitions

STRATEGIES AND TIPS

A **strategy** is a plan. A **tip** is a suggestion. A strategy tells you how to answer a question. A tip will help you answer it quickly.

IELTS exam is a two-hour exam with four parts and many types of questions in each part. You need to have a plan before you start to answer these questions. You need to have a strategy. There are many possible ways to try to answer a question; you must find the best strategy for you.

The tips in this book will help you make efficient choices. The tips will make you a faster, more proficient test taker. A good test strategy combined with useful tips will improve your efficiency and increase your score on the exam.

IELTS Basic Strategies

Key Words

When you search the Internet, you type a word into the web browser. That word is a **key word**. The browser will search all the web pages on the Internet for that word or a related word.

Similarly, you can use key words to help you on the IELTS. You identify a key word in the questions and answers and then search the passage for that word or a related word.

Key words will help you focus your attention on what is important when you read or when you listen. If you look and listen for a key word or a related word, you will be able to find the answer to the question faster.

Key words can be any part of speech, but they are usually nouns, verbs, and modifiers. They answer the questions: *who, what, when, where, why,* and *how*.

READING

STRATEGY	Identify a key word and scan for the key word or related word in the passage.
TIP	Scan for several key words at the same time.

Multiple-Choice Questions

Before you read the passage, read the multiple-choice questions below. The key words are underlined. Then scan the passage looking for key words or related words. These key words are also underlined. Finally, answer the questions.

*Choose the correct letter, **A**, **B**, or **C**.*

1 The wheel was invented
- **A** before making of textiles.
- **B** during the Bronze Age.
- **C** after 3500 BC.

2 The earliest evidence shows wheels being used to
- **A** make pottery.
- **B** move carts.
- **C** run machinery.

3 Wheels were used on toy animals in ancient
- **A** Poland.
- **B** Mesopotamia.
- **C** Mexico.

The wheel is one of the most important technological developments of human civilization. Even so, it wasn't invented until the Bronze Age and was preceded by many other important technological innovations such as making textiles, boats, pottery, and musical instruments.

We tend to think of the wheel as a means of transportation, but its uses go far beyond helping carts and cars roll. In addition to innovations such as water wheels and spinning wheels, wheels in the form of gears and other spinning parts are vital components in countless types of machines. In fact, the first recorded use of the wheel was actually a potter's wheel. Clay tablets from ancient Mesopotamia show evidence that potter's wheels were in use as early as 3500 BC. This is several hundred years before wheels were first used on chariots for transportation.

It is not certain where the use of wheels on carts and chariots originated. At one time, Mesopotamia was considered to be the birthplace of wheeled transportation, but recent evidence points to Europe as a likely place. Early images of carts have been discovered in Poland and other nearby areas, while linguistic evidence suggests that Ukraine was the place where wheeled carts were first used.

Wherever the wheel originated, its use spread throughout the Middle East and Europe from about 3300 BC on. It did not, however, develop among the ancient cultures of the Americas. Or rather it did, but only in the form of toys. Excavations in Mexico in the 1940s revealed small ceramic dogs and other animals that had wheels for legs, and it is assumed that these were used as children's toys. One possible reason that these cultures did not develop the wheel for transportation is that they did not have any domestic animals that were large enough to pull wheeled wagons.

Explanation

1. **Answer: B.** The second sentence of the first paragraph contains most of the key words in question #1. This sentence tells us that the wheel was invented in the Bronze Age (... *it wasn't invented until the Bronze Age* ...), after, not before, sewing and weaving (... *was preceded by* ... *sewing and weaving* ...). The key word *3500 BC* appears in the next paragraph, in a different context.
2. **Answer: A.** The key words and related words for question #2 appear in the second paragraph. The phrase *first recorded use* means the same as *earliest evidence*, so we know the answer to the question will be found near it. The phrase *potter's wheel* in the same sentence tells us that the earliest evidence shows wheels being used for making pottery.
3. **Answer: C.** Two of the key words for question #3, *Mesopotamia* and *Poland*, both appear in the third paragraph; however, the key word that the question asks about, *toy animals*, is not in that paragraph. The other answer choice, *Mexico*, appears in the fourth paragraph and the key word *toy animals* also appears there. This is where the wheeled toys of ancient Mexico are described.

Short-Answer Questions

Before you read the passage, read the short-answer questions below. The key words are underlined. Then scan the passage looking for key words or related words. These key words are also underlined. Finally, answer the questions.

Write ***NO MORE THAN THREE WORDS AND/OR A NUMBER*** *for each answer.*

1 On what date did the fire begin? ....

2 How many people died in the fire? ....

3 Where did the fire start? ....

One of the worst disasters in the nineteenth-century United States was the Great Chicago Fire of 1871. The fire raged through the city from the evening of October 8 until the early hours of October 10, when a rainfall finally helped extinguish it. By that time, the fire had swept through an area of about nine square kilometers, destroying everything in its path: houses, apartment buildings, streets, sidewalks, even lampposts. Property damage was estimated at around 200 million dollars, and over 100,000 people (out of the city's total population of 300,000) were left homeless. Three hundred people lost their lives, a relatively small number for such a large fire.

The first alarm notifying the fire department of the fire was pulled at a pharmacy at 9:40 in the evening. The origin of the fire has been famously traced to Mrs. O'Leary's barn. However, the popular legend that has the fire being started when Mrs. O'Leary's cow kicked over a kerosene lantern is simply not true. A newspaper reporter later admitted to having invented that story for its sensationalistic value. Nevertheless, it was determined that the fire did begin in Mrs. O'Leary's barn, although the exact cause remains unknown. Interestingly enough, Mrs. O'Leary's house, just in front of her barn, escaped damage.

Explanation

1. **Answer: October 8.** There are two dates in the first paragraph: *October 8*, the beginning date of the fire, and *October 10*, the end date.
2. **Answer: Three hundred.** When answering a *How many* question, look for numbers. There are several numbers about people near the end of the first paragraph. Also in the last sentence of that paragraph, we have the phrase *lost their lives*, which means the same as *died.* That is the sentence that tells us the answer to the question.

3. **Answer: Mrs. O'Leary's barn.** When answering a *Where* question, look for places. There are several places mentioned in the second paragraph: a pharmacy, Mrs. O'Leary's barn, and Mrs. O'Leary's house. The second sentence contains key words *origin* (meaning *beginning*) and *Mrs. O'Leary's barn*. The second to the last sentence contains key words *begin* and *Mrs. O'Leary's barn*. Both these sentences state that the fire began in Mrs. O'Leary's barn.

PRACTICE 1 (answers begin on page 197)

Before you look at each passage, read the questions and underline the key words. Then scan the passage and underline the key word or related word. Finally, answer the questions.

Passage 1

Oceans make up over seventy percent of the Earth's surface. But an ocean is more than just a large area of water. Oceans consist of several zones with different conditions, providing habitat for a variety of plant and animal species. The littoral zone is the area where the ocean meets the land. This zone consists of several subzones: land that is only underwater when there are super high tides such as during a storm (the supralittoral zone), the area that is submerged when the tide is high and exposed when the tide is low (the intertidal zone), and the area below the low tide line that is always underwater (the sublittoral zone). Snails, crabs, and small fish as well as various types of seaweed are all inhabitants of this part of the ocean.

The pelagic zone is the area farther out from the shore. This zone covers most of the ocean, excepting the areas close to shore and near the ocean floor. The top 200 meters of this zone is where sunlight is most abundant and is home to the highest diversity of plant and animal species in the ocean. In addition to various seaweeds and fishes, marine mammals such as whales and dolphins also inhabit this area and feed on the abundant plankton.

As you move into the deeper waters, less and less sunlight is able to penetrate the water. In the benthic zone, near the ocean floor, there is no light at all, and photosynthesis cannot take place. Animals that live here are scavengers, getting their nutrition from dead and dying organisms that float down from the upper regions of the water.

Classify the following phrases as describing

A the littoral zone
B the pelagic zone
C the benthic zone

1 the area along the shore
2 the area at the bottom of the ocean
3 home to crabs and snails
4 home to sea mammals
5 has the greatest variety of plant and animal types
6 inhabitants eat dead animals

Passage 2

The use of wheeled carts in the ancient world was limited by the fact that to be truly useful they needed smooth roads. The ancient Romans are renowned for the stone roads they constructed all over Europe, beginning in 312 BC with the Appian Way. This 260-kilometer road connected Rome with the city of Taranto. As more and more territory came under Roman control, roads were built throughout the empire, extending from Rome to what is today Great Britain, Romania, North Africa, and Iraq. These roads facilitated all types of travel, wheeled or not.

Wooden work carts were common throughout Europe for centuries. In fact, they were the major mode of wheeled transportation until the 1500s, when Hungarians began to build coaches. With smooth, finished wood and soft, cushioned seats, coaches provided a much more comfortable ride than rough wooden carts. Their popularity spread across the continent. In the following centuries, various styles of coaches, carriages, and wagons were developed to provide transportation for all types of situations.

Directions

Do the following statements agree with the information given in the passage?
On your Answer Sheet write

TRUE *if the statement agrees with the information in the passage*
FALSE *if the statement contradicts the information in the passage*
NOT GIVEN *if there is no information about this in the passage*

1 The Appian Way was the first stone road built by the ancient Romans.

2 The Appian Way led from Rome to Great Britain.

3 The Appian Way was the most heavily used Roman road.

4 Ancient Roman roads were used only by travelers in wheeled carts.

5 The first European coaches were made in Hungary.

Passage 3

Choose the correct heading for each section, ***A–D****, from the list of headings below.*

List of Headings

i Reasons to Use Wind Power
ii Wind Power in the Twentieth Century
iii Arguments Against Wind Power
iv Wind Power in Early History

1 Section **A**

2 Section **B**

3 Section **C**

4 Section **D**

A

People have been harnessing the power of the wind for centuries. The first documented use of wind power was in Persia about 1500 years ago, where windmills were used to pump water and grind grain. Windmills may actually have been in use in China earlier than this; however, the first documented use of wind power there was in the thirteenth century, again for pumping water and grinding grain. Windmills were also being used in Europe at the same time and were an important source of power for several centuries. Their use eventually declined in the nineteenth century with the introduction of the steam engine.

B

Throughout the 1900s, the development and use of windmills was focused on the generation of electricity. In the early part of the century, wind-generated electricity was widely used in the Midwestern United States. As the demand for electricity grew and the electrical grid was extended through that part of the country, wind power fell out of use. In the latter part of the century, there was a renewed interest in wind power as an alternative to the use of fossil fuels to generate electricity.

C

In the twenty-first century, the use of wind-generated electricity is growing as many see the benefits of this source of power. In addition to reducing dependency on fossil fuels, wind power is also clean and inexpensive to use. The wind, after all, is free. Wind turbines can be built on open farmland, thus providing the farmer with another source of income. Wind turbines don't occupy a large amount of space, and the land around them can be cultivated.

D

As with anything, however, there are also drawbacks. Although using wind turbines is inexpensive, the initial investment required to construct them is quite high. Wind turbines have to be located where they can capture the wind, often on high mountain ridges or in open areas free of obstacles, such as tall buildings. This means they are usually located away from population centers where the most electricity is needed. So there is the additional cost of installing lines to transmit the electricity to cities. Some people are concerned about the high level of noise spinning wind turbines create. Others are concerned about the effect on wildlife, especially birds, which have been killed by flying into the turbines.

Passage 4

As with anything, however, there are also drawbacks. Although using wind turbines is inexpensive, the initial investment required to construct them is quite high. Wind turbines have to be located where they can capture the wind, often on high mountain ridges or in open areas free of obstacles, such as tall buildings. This means they are usually located away from population centers where the most electricity is needed. So there is the additional cost of installing lines to transmit the electricity to cities. Some people are concerned about the high level of noise spinning wind turbines create. Others are concerned about the effect on wildlife, especially birds, which have been killed by flying into the turbines.

*Which **FOUR** disadvantages of wind power are mentioned in the passage?*

A Wind turbines can cause harm to animals.
B Wind turbines in a rural landscape can spoil the scenery.
C The best wind turbine sites are usually far from cities.
D It costs a lot to build wind turbines.
E Wind speed is not reliable.
F Wind turbines are very noisy.
G Wind turbines don't generate as much electricity as fossil fuel power stations do.

Passage 5

Psychologist Jean Piaget identified four stages in the intellectual development of children, from birth to about twelve years of age. He identified the ages at which most children pass through each stage and the concepts and abilities they develop. While he acknowledged that children may go through each stage at different rates or at somewhat different ages, he was firm in his belief that the cognitive development of all children always follows the same sequence.

According to Piaget, children from birth to around two years of age are in the sensorimotor stage of development. During this stage, children learn how objects can be manipulated. They learn that their actions can have an effect on objects. They experiment by touching, holding, or throwing things or by putting them in their mouths and seeing what results. Initially, infants are concerned only with things that are directly before their eyes. During this stage, they develop the concept of object permanence. They learn that things continue to exist even when out of sight.

The preoperational stage is the period from around two to seven years of age. Children in this stage are able to think symbolically. They develop their use of language. They are also very egocentric, assuming that everyone else shares their same point of view. Another characteristic of this stage is animism—the belief that inanimate objects can think and feel in the same way the child does. Thus, a child might feel sorry for a broken toy, for example.

*Choose the correct letter, **A**, **B**, or **C**.*

1 Piaget believed that all children
- **A** learn at the same pace.
- **B** develop cognitive abilities in the same order.
- **C** pass through twelve stages of development.

2 During the sensorimotor stage, infants learn by
- **A** manipulating objects.
- **B** focusing only on what they can see.
- **C** being touched and held by their parents.

3 Children in the preoperational stage
- **A** have very limited use of language.
- **B** are interested in other people's viewpoints.
- **C** believe that things have thoughts and feelings.

LISTENING

STRATEGY Read the questions before you listen. Identify a key word, and then listen for the key word or related word in the passage.

TIP Pay attention to the words following the key word or related word.

Complete Notes

Before you listen to the audio, read the incomplete notes below. The key words have been underlined for you. Then listen to the audio and follow along with the audio text. (You will not see the text during the test. This is only for strategy practice.) As you listen to the audio, note the underlined key words or related words.

Complete the notes below.

*Write **NO MORE THAN THREE WORDS** for each answer.*

Apartments

Luxury Towers
top floor apartment:
* has a **1** ....
all apartments:
* large living room
* separate **2** ....
* eat-in kitchen

Parkview Apartments
* ground floor apartments have a **3** ....
* one available **4** ....

Main Street Apartments
* smallest and most **5** ....

Audio Text

Woman: Our agency has quite a few apartments listed in your price range. So a lot will depend on which part of the city you are interested in.
Man: I'd prefer not to be too far from downtown, or at least close to the subway.
Woman: That gives us several options. You may like Luxury Towers. There are several vacant apartments there now. There is one on the top floor that has a view that's quite spectacular. You can see the harbour very clearly from there.
Man: Great. How big is the apartment?
Woman: All the apartments in the building are quite spacious, and in addition to a large living room, each also has a separate dining room as well as an eat-in kitchen.
Man: I'd definitely like to visit Luxury Towers. But I'd like to look in other buildings, too.
Woman: Parkview Apartments will have some vacancies soon. All the ground floor apartments there have a small patio, which is a very nice feature.
Man: Will any of the ground floor apartments be vacant soon?
Woman: Yes, there will be one available next month. Now, if you'd like to be right downtown, I can show you some apartments on Main Street.
Man: Yes, I'd like to see them.
Woman: They're the smallest apartments I have to show you, but despite that, they're also the most expensive, because of the location, you know.
Man: I think it's still worth looking at.

Explanation

1. **Answer: view.** The categories of the notes *Luxury Towers* and *top floor* are key words. Listen for the answer to question 1 in the discussion of the top floor apartment in Luxury Towers. The words right before the blanks are also key words. For question 1, the key word is *has,* so listen for the answer near that word.
2. **Answer: dining room.** Question 2 comes under the category of *all apartments*, so listen for the answer to that question during the discussion of all apartments in Luxury Towers. Then listen for the key word *separate*. The speaker mentions a separate dining room.
3. **Answer: small patio.** The key words *Parkview Apartments* and *ground floor apartments* signal in which part of the conversation to listen for the answer to this question. Listen for the exact answer near the key word that comes right near the blank, in this case, *have*. The speaker says: *All the ground floor apartments there have a small patio....*
4. **Answer: next month.** Listen for the key word *available*. The speaker says: ... *there will be one available next month*.
5. **Answer: expensive.** In the discussion of Main Street Apartments, listen for the key word *most*. The speaker says: ... *they're also the most expensive....*

Multiple-Choice Questions

Before you listen to the audio, read the multiple-choice questions below. The key words have been underlined for you. Then listen to the audio and follow along with the audio text. (You will not see the text during the test. This is only for strategy practice.) As you listen to the audio, note the underlined key words or related words.

1 Theory X and Theory Y explain
- **A** employees' behavior.
- **B** managers' perceptions.
- **C** psychologists' motivation.

2 According to Theory X, workers
- **A** enjoy their jobs.
- **B** seek out more responsibility.
- **C** need constant supervision.

3 According to Theory Y, workers
- **A** motivate themselves.
- **B** avoid decision making.
- **C** prefer a hierarchical workplace.

Theory X and Theory Y are theories of motivation in the workplace developed by social psychologist Douglas McGregor in the 1960s. They describe how managers may perceive their employees rather than how employees actually act.

A Theory X manager assumes that workers are not motivated and dislike their jobs. Therefore, they have to be controlled and supervised every step of the way or they will not carry out their duties. They avoid responsibility or taking on any extra work. Workplaces that ascribe to Theory X are hierarchical with many levels of managers and supervisors to keep the workers under control.

Theory Y describes the opposite situation. This theory assumes that employees are self-motivated and enjoy their work, that they want greater responsibility and don't need a lot of supervision. Theory Y managers believe that their employees want to do well at work and that, given the right conditions, they will. In a Theory Y workplace, even lower-level employees are involved in decision making.

Explanation

1. **Answer: B.** This question asks what Theory X and Theory Y are about, which is explained at the beginning of the talk. The last sentence of this part of the talk answers the question. It tells us that these theories are about manager's perceptions (related word: *perceive*), not about how employees act (related word: *behavior*).
2. **Answer: C.** The second part of the talk describes Theory X. According to this theory, workers have to be supervised. We know that choice A is wrong because the talk says the opposite (related word: *dislike*). Workers enjoying their jobs is part of the Theory Y description in the next part of the talk. We know that choice B is wrong because the talk says the opposite: Workers avoid responsibility. Workers seeking out responsibility is part of the Theory Y description.
3. **Answer: A.** The third part of the talk describes Theory Y. Theory Y describes employees as self motivated (related words: *workers, motivate themselves*). Choice B contains key words *decision making*. These are discussed near the end of the talk, but the speaker says that employees are involved in this, not that they *avoid* it. Choice C key word *hierarchical* is part of the discussion of Theory X.

PRACTICE 2 (answers begin on page 202)

Before you listen to the audio, read the questions. Underline the key words. Then listen to the audio and pay attention to the key words and related words. Answer the questions as you hear the answers.

Passage 1

Label the map below.

*Write **NO MORE THAN TWO WORDS** for each answer.*

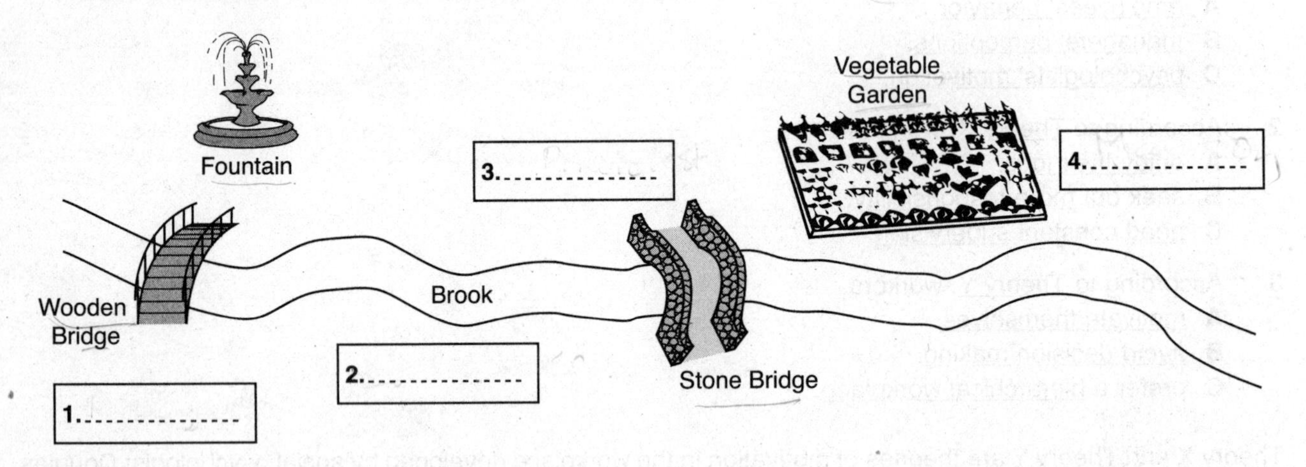

Passage 2

What will the students include in their presentation?

A They definitely will include this.
B They might include this.
C They will not include this.

*Write the correct letter, **A, B,** or **C**.*

1 a guest speaker
2 charts and graphs
3 photographs
4 interview transcripts
5 their questionnaire

In the answer key on page 202, you will find the key words for the map, the questions, and the audio text underlined. Use the answer key to practice your key word strategies.

Passage 3

Complete the table below.

*Write **NO MORE THAN TWO WORDS** for each answer.*

Advantages	**Disadvantages**
People will be more likely to recycle because the system is so **1**	Some residents are angry because they **2** .... the system.
It costs little to **3** .... recyclables from residences.	The cost of building the **4** .... is high.

Passage 4

Complete the form below.

*Write **NO MORE THAN THREE WORDS AND/OR A NUMBER** for each answer.*

Piano Rentals Unlimited

Client Information Form

Name: Patricia **1** ....

Address: **2** ....

Instrument requested: upright piano

Delivery date: **3** ....

Length of rental: **4** ....

Payment method: **5** ....

Passage 5

*Choose **FOUR** letters, **A–G**.*

*Which **FOUR** things should trip participants bring from home?*

A bicycles
B water bottles
C maps
D food
E hats
F tents
G cameras

IELTS Basic Tips

There are some basic tips that will help you in all sections of the IELTS.

Directions

Always read the directions carefully. Do exactly what the question asks. Pay special attention to the number of words you can write. Do not write more than the number of words specified.

Guessing

Answer every question. If you don't answer a question, you will receive no point for that question. But if you guess, you have a chance of getting the right answer.

Time

Keep moving through the questions. Don't take too much time with a question. You can come back later. If you don't know an answer, guess.

Question/Answer Sequence

The questions follow the order of the passage, talk, or conversation, but the answer options do not. The answer options might be in a different order.

Spelling

Spelling is important. All words must be spelled correctly. Check your answers to make sure the words are spelled correctly. A good study practice is to listen to the audio recordings in this book and write what you hear. Then check your spelling in the audio transcript section.

IELTS Study Contract

You must make a commitment to study English. Sign a contract with yourself. A contract is a formal agreement to do something. You should not break a contract—especially a contract with yourself.

- Print your name below on line 1.
- Write the time you will spend each week studying English on lines 4–8. Think about how much time you have to study everyday and every week, and make your schedule realistic.
- Sign your name and date the contract on the last line.
- At the end of each week, add up your hours. Did you meet the requirements of your contract?

IELTS STUDY CONTRACT

I, ... , promise to study for the IELTS. I will begin my study with *Barron's IELTS Strategies and Tips*, and I will also study English on my own.

I understand that to improve my English I need to spend time on English.

I promise to study English .... a week.

I will spend .... hours a week listening to English.
I will spend .... hours a week writing English.
I will spend .... hours a week speaking English.
I will spend .... hours a week reading English.

This is a contract with myself. I promise to fulfill the terms of this contract.

____

Signed

____

Date

Self-Study Activities

Here are some ways you can improve your English skills on your own. Check the ones you plan to try. Add some of your own ideas.

Internet Based Self-Study Activities

LISTENING

.... Podcasts on the Internet
.... News websites: CNN, BBC, NBC, ABC, CBS
.... Movies in English
.... You Tube
.... Lectures on the Internet
....
....

WRITING

.... Write e-mails to website contacts
.... Write a blog
.... Leave comments on blogs
.... Post messages in a chat room
.... Use Facebook and MySpace
....
....

SPEAKING

.... Use Skype to talk to English speakers
....
....

READING

.... Read news and magazine articles online
.... Do web research on topics that interest you
.... Follow blogs that interest you
....
....

Other Self-Study Activities

LISTENING

.... Listen to CNN and BBC on the radio

.... Watch movies and TV in English

.... Listen to music in English

....

....

SPEAKING

.... Describe what you see and do out loud

.... Practice speaking with a conversation buddy

....

....

WRITING

.... Write a daily journal

.... Write a letter to an English speaker

.... Make lists of the things you see everyday

.... Write descriptions of your family and friends

.... Summarize news items or sports events that you've read about online

....

....

READING

.... Read newspapers and magazines in English

.... Read books in English

....

....

Examples of Self-Study Activities

Whether you read an article in a newspaper or on a website, you can use that article in a variety of ways to improve your vocabulary while you practice reading, writing, speaking, and listening in English.

- Read about it.
- Paraphrase and write about it.
- Give a talk or presentation about it.
- Record or make a video of your presentation.
- Listen to or watch what you recorded. Write down your presentation.
- Correct your mistakes.
- Do it all again.

Plan a Trip

Go to *www.concierge.com*

Choose a city, choose a hotel, go to that hotel's website and choose a room, and then choose some sites to visit (*reading*). Write a report about the city. Tell why you want to go there. Describe the hotel and the room you will reserve. Tell what sites you plan to visit and when. Where will you eat? How will you get around?

Now write a letter to someone recommending this place (*writing*). Pretend you have to give a lecture on your planned trip (*speaking*). Make a video of yourself talking about this place. Then watch the video and write down what you said. Correct any mistakes you made and record the presentation again. Then choose another city and do this again.

Shop for an Electronic Product

Go to *www.cnet.com*

Choose an electronic product and read about it (*reading*). Write a report about the product. Tell why you want to buy one. Describe its features.

Now write a letter to someone recommending this product, or think of a problem you might have with this type of product and write a letter of complaint to the company. Don't send the letter, this is just an exercise (*writing*). Pretend you have to give a talk about this product (*speaking*). Make a video of yourself talking about this product. Then watch the video and write down what you said. Correct any mistakes you made and record the presentation again. Now choose another product and do this again.

Discuss a Book or a CD

Go to *www.amazon.com*

Choose a book or record or any product. Read the product description and reviews (*reading*). Write a report about the product. Tell why you want to buy one or why it is interesting to you. Describe its features.

Now write a letter to someone recommending this product (*writing*). Pretend you have to give a talk about this product (*speaking*). Make a video of yourself talking about this product. Then watch the video and write down what you said. Correct any mistakes you made and record the presentation again. Then choose another product and do this again.

Discuss Any Subject

Go to *http://simple.wikipedia.org/wiki/Main_Page*

This website is written in simple English. Pick any subject and read the entry (*reading*).

Write a short essay about the topic (*writing*). Give a presentation about it (*speaking*). Record the presentation. Then watch the video and write down what you said. Correct any mistakes you made and record the presentation again. Choose another topic and do this again.

Discuss Any Event

Go to *http://news.google.com*

Google News has a variety of links. Pick one event and read the articles about it (*reading*).

Write a short essay about the event (*writing*). Give a presentation about it (*speaking*). Record the presentation. Then watch the video and write down what you said. Correct any mistakes you made and record the presentation again. Now choose another event and do this again.

Report the News

Listen to an English language news report on the radio or watch a news program on TV (*listening*). Take notes as you listen. Write a summary of what you heard (*writing*).

Pretend you are a news reporter. Use the information from your notes to report the news (*speaking*). Record the presentation. Then watch the video and write down what you said. Correct any mistakes you made and record the presentation again. Now listen to another news program and do this again.

Express an Opinion

Read a letter to the editor in the newspaper (*reading*). Write a letter in response in which you say whether or not you agree with the opinion expressed in the first letter. Explain why (*writing*).

Pretend you have to give a talk explaining your opinion (*speaking*). Record yourself giving the talk. Then watch the video and write down what you said. Correct any mistakes you made and record the presentation again. Now read another letter to the editor and do this again.

Review a Book or Movie

Read a book (*reading*). Think about your opinion of the book. What did you like about it? What didn't you like about it? Who would you recommend it to and why? Pretend you are a book reviewer for a newspaper. Write a review of the book with your opinion and recommendations (*writing*).

Give an oral presentation about the book. Explain what the book is about and what your opinion is (*speaking*). Record yourself giving the presentation. Then watch the video and write down what you said. Correct any mistakes you made and record the presentation again. Now read another book and do this again.

You can do this same activity after watching a movie (*listening*).

Summarize a TV Show

Watch a TV show in English (*listening*). Take notes as you listen. After watching, write a summary of the show (*writing*).

Use your notes to give an oral summary of the show. Explain the characters, setting, and plot (*speaking*). Record yourself speaking. Then watch the video and write down what you said. Correct any mistakes you made and record the presentation again. Now watch another TV show and do this again.

Listen to a Lecture

Listen to an academic or other type of lecture on the Internet. Go to any of the following or similar sites and look for lectures on topics that are of interest to you:

http://lecturefox.com
http://freevideolectures.com
http://podcasts.ox.ac.uk
http://www.ted.com/talks

Listen to a lecture and take notes as you listen. Listen again to check and add to your notes (*listening*). Use your notes to write a summary of the lecture (*writing*).

Pretend you have to give a lecture on the same subject. Use your notes to give your lecture (*speaking*). Record yourself as you lecture. Then watch the video and write down what you said. Correct any mistakes you made and record the lecture again. Now listen to another lecture and do this again.

IELTS LISTENING MODULE

OVERVIEW

In this chapter, you will learn and practice specific strategies based on the various types of questions you may see in the Listening Module. Although each of the question types is presented here in the context of one of the four sections of the Listening Module, most of them can appear in any section of the module. In this chapter you will also practice the key word strategies you learned in the first chapter of the book. At the end of this chapter, you will find a Strategy Review that is similar to the actual IELTS Listening test.

GENERAL STRATEGIES

Listening for Words
Listening for Numbers

SPECIFIC STRATEGIES

SECTION 1—CONVERSATION

Complete a Form
Complete a Table
Choose Answers from a List

SECTION 2—TALK

Complete Sentences
Label a Diagram, Plan, or Map
Give a Short Answer

SECTION 3—DISCUSSION

Choose Answer from Multiple Choices
Label a Diagram
Match Words and Phrases

SECTION 4—TALK OR LECTURE

Classify Words or Statements
Complete Notes
Complete a Flowchart

STRATEGY REVIEW

Listening Tip

Nothing is repeated in the Listening Module. If you miss an answer, you will not have a chance to go back and listen for the answer again. Don't waste time worrying about it. Just keep moving ahead. Answer all the questions that you can.

General Strategies

Listening for Words

STRATEGY	Use the questions to focus your attention on the key words as you listen. (See pages 1–11 for a discussion and activities on Key Words.)
TIP	Key words are often stressed. Listen for words that are stressed.

PRACTICE 1 (answers on page 206)

Here are the directions for the exercises Audio 1—Audio 4. For each audio exercise, look at the questions and circle the key words. Then read the script once and make predictions about the words in the gaps, but don't complete them yet. Next, read the script again as you listen to the audio and complete the gaps. Finally, answer the questions.

Audio 1

*Choose **TWO** letters.*

Which **TWO** things are included in the price of the hotel room?

A breakfast
B use of an exercise room
C use of a swimming pool
D afternoon tea
E movies

Script

Woman: A room for two people is two hundred fifty dollars a night.
Man: That seems a bit high.

Woman: The rooms are very comfortable. And we serve **1**...................... to all our guests every morning from seven to nine.
Man: That sounds nice. Do you have an **2** ....?

Woman: No, but there is a club across the street you can use, for a **3** .... We do have our own **4**................, which guests can use **5** ....
Man: Oh, that's good. I'll certainly use that. Do you serve other meals besides breakfast?

Woman: Yes, we serve three meals a day, plus 6................. . The menu and 7......................... are available on our website if you'd like to see them.

Man: Oh, OK. I'll take a look at it.

Woman: You might also like to know that each room has a large screen TV, and for an 8................. you can order 9.................. .

Audio 2

*Choose the correct letter, **A**, **B**, or **C**.*

1 Where will they have lunch?
- **A** in the park
- **B** by the river
- **C** near the museum

2 What will they do immediately after lunch?
- **A** visit the museum
- **B** take a walk
- **C** go shopping

Script

Welcome to Urban Tours. We'll begin our tour today with a bus ride through **1**................, which is known for its landscaping and gardens. We'll spend an hour walking through the park's Central Flower garden, which is in full bloom this time of year. Then we'll get back on the bus and ride over the **2**................ and on to the **3**................. Before visiting the museum, we'll enjoy **4**................ at Shell's Café, located just **5**................, and then take a **6**................ through the neighborhood to view some historic buildings. Then we'll enjoy a special **7**................ of the museum, and we'll have an hour or two after that to visit the nearby **8**................ where you can make any **9**................ you want before returning to the hotel.

Audio 3

What does Bob say about his classes?

Choose your answers from the box.

A	It's his favorite class.
B	It's not interesting.
C	It's very difficult.
D	It's too big.

1 chemistry
2 math
3 psychology

Script

Man:	I have a really tough schedule this semester.
Woman:	You're taking some **1**................ classes, aren't you?
Man:	It's not that so much, but I think I chose the wrong courses. My **2**................, for example, has way **3**................ in it.
Woman:	Really?
Man:	Yeah. It's impossible to ask a question or get any attention from the instructor because of that.
Woman:	What about your **4**................? You were really looking forward to taking that.
Man:	I was, but, like I said, I chose the wrong class. I never knew **5**................ could be **6**................ .
Woman:	That's too bad. So I guess you feel like this semester is a complete waste.
Man:	Actually, no. Believe it or not, I'm really enjoying my **7**................ . I like it **8**................ of all my classes.

Audio 4

Which features are characteristic of which animal?

Choose the correct letter.

A	Rabbit
B	Hare

1 Its babies are blind. ....

2 It lives in groups. ....

3 It lives above ground. ....

4 Its diet consists of woody plants. ....

5 Its diet consists of soft vegetation. ....

Script

Although rabbits and hares are very similar in appearance, they are different animals with different characteristics. We can say that the differences start at birth. **1**................ are able to defend themselves, at least to some degree, because they **2**............... when they are born. When **3**..............., however, they **4**................ and so are completely helpless. Unlike hares, rabbits stick together, living with other rabbits in colonies. They live in **5**..............., which provide a safe place to hide from predators. Hares, on the other hand, live most of their lives as loners. They stay **6**................ and are able to avoid predators because they are such good runners. Hares and rabbits also have different **7**................ . Hares tend to favor bark, twigs, and other **8**................ while rabbits prefer **9**..............., leaves, and stems.

Listening for Numbers

STRATEGY Be familiar with the different ways to express numbers.

TIP Make a note whenever you hear a number. Note that in a long number the intonation rises and then falls at the last number.

↑↑↓ ↑↑↓ ↑↑↑↓
505-475-3948

Whether the number is an identification number, a date, or a price, there are a variety of ways the number can be said.

Dates: November 24, 2013
November twenty-fourth, two thousand thirteen
November twenty-four, twenty thirteen

Price: $13.33
Thirteen dollars and thirty-three cents
Thirteen thirty three

Time: 2:45
Two forty-five
Quarter to two
A quarter to two

Decimals: 3.75
Three point seven five
Three and three-fourths
Three and three-quarters

Telephone numbers / Credit card numbers / ID numbers:
+1 505 475-3948
Plus one five-o-five four seven five, three nine, four eight.
Plus one five zero five, four seventy-five, thirty-nine forty-eight

PRACTICE 2 (answers on page 207)

Write the numbers, dates, and times you hear.

1 ....

2 ....

3 ....

4 ....

5 ....

6 ....

7 ....

8 ....

9 ....

10 ....

11 ....

12 ....

13 ....

14 ....

15 ....

Specific Strategies

SECTION 1—CONVERSATION
Complete a Form

STRATEGY Pay attention to the words before and after the gap. Listen, in this example, for these words: *Name* and *Address,* which appear before the gap.

Name: **1** .... Jones

Address: 154 **2**................

TIP The order of the gaps in the form will follow the conversation.

PRACTICE 1 (answers on page 207)

Circle the key words around the gaps. Then listen to the conversation and complete each form. Write ***NO MORE THAN THREE WORDS AND/OR A NUMBER*** *for each answer.*

Conversation 1

Argyle Car Rentals

Name: William **1** ....

Address: 17 North Cameron Street, Compton

License Number: **2** ....

Insurance Company: **3** ....

Type of car: **4** ....

Pick up date: **5** ....

Payment method: credit card

Conversation 2

Ticket Order Form

Name: Petronella Jones

Show date: **1** ...., March 10

Show time: **2** ....

Number of tickets: **3** ....

Seat location: **4** ....

Notes: **5** .... discount

pick up __ mail X

Conversation 3

Sanditon Hotel
Reservation Form

Guest name: **1** .... Wiggins

Arrival date: June 23

Length of stay: **2** ....

Room type: **3** ....

Room preferences: **4** .... view

Credit card number: **5** ....

Conversation 4

Westfield Language Academy
Student Registration Form

Name: Ronald McGraw

Address: **1** ....

Phone: **2** ....

Course title: **3** ....

Days: **4** ....

Payment method: **5** ....

Conversation 5

Student Employment Office

Name: Shirley Chang

Address: PO Box **1** ...., Bradford

Date available: **2** ....

Job type: **3** ....

Previous experience: **4** ....

Skills: **5** ....

Complete a Table

STRATEGY	Read the headings in the table and decide what you are listening for.
TIP	The missing words will be the same as the other words in the column.

CLASS SCHEDULE

↓ Classroom	↓ Course	↓ Days	↓ Time
Room 10	**1**	Monday, Wednesday	10:30–11:30 AM
Room 25	Chemistry	**2**	1:00–2:30 PM
Room 45	Physics	Wednesday, Friday	**3** ....

If the gap appears in a column of course titles, the missing word is a course title. If the gap appears in a column of days, the missing word is a day of the week. If the gap appears in a column of time, the missing word is a time of day.

PRACTICE 2 (answers on page 207)

Circle the headings. Guess the type of word you will provide. Then listen to the conversation and complete the table. Write ***NO MORE THAN THREE WORDS AND/OR A NUMBER*** *for each answer.*

Conversation 1

Westfield Language Academy—Spring Schedule

Course Title	Days	Cost	Ages
1	Monday and Wednesday	$575	Adults over 18
Advanced Spanish	Tuesday	**2** $	Adults over 18
Beginning Chinese	**3**	$325	Children **4** ....
Beginning French	**5**	$325	Children 6–10

Conversation 2

City Arts Center—Calendar of Events

Date	Time	Event	Ticket Price	Location
August 10	10 AM–8 PM	**1**	$35	Circle Theater
August 11	9 AM–5 PM	Crafts Fair	$5	**2** ....
August 17	8 PM	Play: *Romeo and Juliet*	**3** $....................	Starlight Theater
August 24	**4** .... PM	**5**	$18	Rigby Hall

Conversation 3

Student Employment Office—Job Listings

Employer	Job	Start date	Salary
Restaurant	**1**	October 15	$18/hour
Clothing store	Bookkeeper	**2**	$21/hour
3	Receptionist	October 23	**4** $........./hour
5	Administrative Assistant	November 2	$13/hour

Conversation 4

Argyle Car Rentals

Vehicle Type	Maximum # of Passengers	Rental Fee (per day)	Special Features
Compact car	four	**1** $	Roof rack
Mid-size car	**2**	$50	**3** ....
4	eight	$75	DVD player
Small truck	four	$85	**5** ....

Conversation 5

Tours

Place	Activity	Length	Transportation
Art museum	view paintings	two hours	**1** ....
National Park	**2**	four hours	bus
3	visit monuments	**4** .... hours	walking
Grover Mansion	house tour	two hours	**5** ....

Talk 3

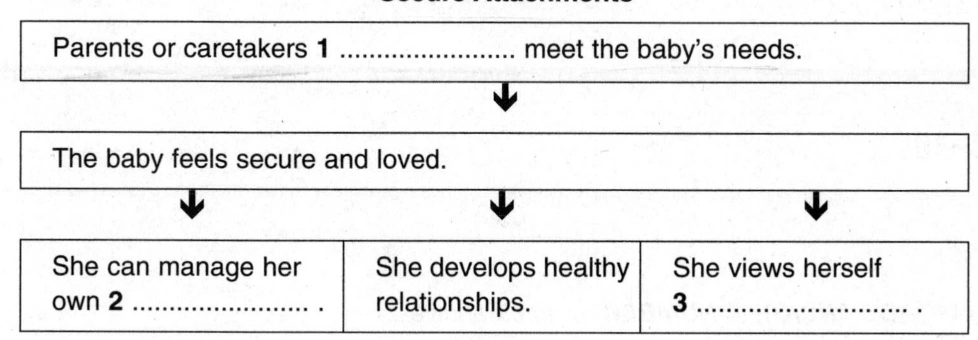
Secure Attachments
Parents or caretakers 1 .... meet the baby's needs.
The baby feels secure and loved.
She can manage her own 2 ....
She develops healthy relationships.
She views herself 3 ....

STRATEGY REVIEW

(answers on page 211)

SECTION 1—QUESTIONS 1–10

Questions 1–4

Complete the form below.

Write ***NO MORE THAN TWO WORDS AND/OR A NUMBER*** *for each answer.*

Lakeside Rentals

Name:	Gregory Thornton
Address:	Box 7, **1**........................, Connecticut
No. in group	**2** ....
Arrival date	**3** ....
Length of stay	**4** ....

Questions 5–8

Complete the table below.

Write ***NO MORE THAN ONE WORD AND/OR A NUMBER*** *for each answer.*

Name	No. of Bedrooms	Special Features	Weekly Rental
5 ...... Cottage	2	porch	$700
Maple Cottage	2	lake view	**6** $...........
Hemlock Cottage	3	**7**	$925
Spruce Cottage	**8**	garden	$900

Questions 9–10

Choose ***TWO*** *letters,* ***A–E****.*

Which TWO activities is Mr. Thornton interested in?

A water skiing
B paddling a canoe
C horseback riding
D tennis
E hiking

SECTION 2—QUESTIONS 11–20

Questions 11–12

*Choose the correct letter, **A**, **B**, or **C**.*

11 When is the zoo closed?
- **A** all holidays
- **B** the first Monday of the month
- **C** the final week of the year

12 What benefit do groups of ten or more get?
- **A** a lower entrance fee
- **B** free entrance to the zoo
- **C** entrance before opening time

Questions 13–17

Label the map below.

*Write the correct letter, **A–F**, next to questions 13–17.*

13 education building ....

14 picnic area ....

15 water birds ....

16 small mammal house ....

17 reptile house ....

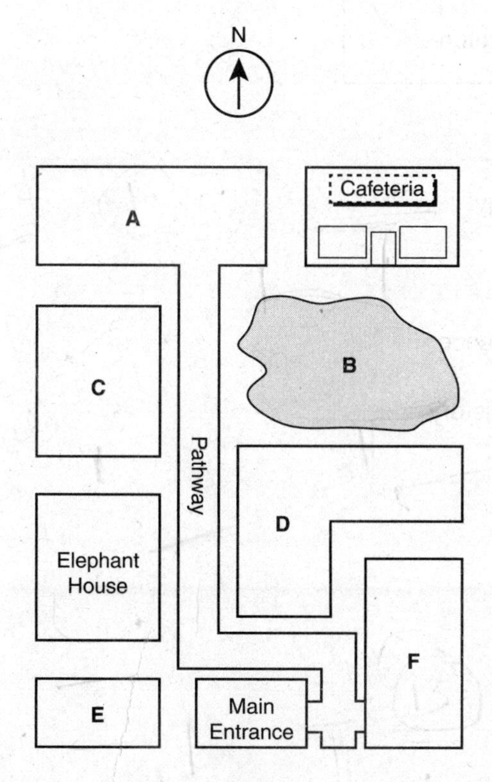

Questions 18–20

*Choose the correct letter, **A**, **B**, or **C**.*

18 The zoo currently has programs for children aged
- **A** 4–5.
- **B** 6–10.
- **C** 12–13.

19 Children are allowed to
- **A** feed the animals.
- **B** pet the animals.
- **C** groom the animals.

20 Teachers are required to
- **A** provide reading materials.
- **B** develop a test.
- **C** remain with their students.

SECTION 3—QUESTIONS 21–30

Questions 21–26

When does Samantha take each of the following classes?

*Write the correct letter, **A**, **B**, or **C**, next to questions 21–26.*

A	She has already taken it.
B	She is taking it now.
C	She plans to take it in the future.

21 .... Biology

22 .... Anthropology

23 .... Economics

24 .... Political Science

25 .... American History

26 .... Literature

Questions 27–30

*Choose the correct letter, **A**, **B**, or **C**.*

27 How does Samantha get to class every day?
A on foot
B by bus
C in a car

28 Where is Samantha working now?
A in an office
B in a bookstore
C in a cafeteria

29 What does Samantha say about this semester?
A It's difficult.
B It's boring.
C It's fun.

30 What will Samantha do during the summer?
A travel
B study
C work

SECTION 4—QUESTIONS 31–40

Complete the notes below.

*Write **NO MORE THAN TWO WORDS** for each answer.*

DOLPHINS AND PORPOISES

True whales don't have **31** ....
A killer whale is the biggest **32** ....
Porpoises are less than **33** .... long.

Nose
A dolphin's is **34** ....
A porpoise's is **35** ....

Teeth
A dolphin's are shaped like **36** ....
A porpoise's are shaped like **37** ....

Dorsal Fin
A dolphin's is **38** ....
A porpoise's is straight.

Other Information
There are just six **39** .... of porpoises.
Dolphins make **40** .... to talk with each other, while porpoises do not.

IELTS READING MODULE

OVERVIEW

In this chapter, you will learn and practice specific strategies based on the various question types. These strategies will introduce you to the types of questions on the Reading Module. You will learn how to answer these questions quickly and correctly. Most of the reading passages in this chapter are shorter than the actual reading passages you will see on the IELTS. They are intended to give you focused practice with the strategies. In the Strategies Review section, you will read passages that are the same length as the passages on the IELTS.

In this chapter, you will review the basic IELTS strategies that you learned in the first chapter of this book. You will learn how these strategies apply directly to the Reading Module.

At the end of this chapter, you will find a Strategy Review that is similar to the actual IELTS Reading test.

Reading Tip

Time is not your friend on the reading test. You must read quickly and diligently to answer all the questions. There are forty questions in the Reading Module. You have one hour to read three passages and answer forty questions.

When you take practice tests, pay attention to how long you spend on each section of the Reading Module. Divide your time and use the time limits in the chart below as a goal. Generally, the passages go from easiest to hardest, so it is better to spend less time on the first passages and more time on the last one.

Passage	Total Time	Skim the Passage	Scan for Answers
1	18	1 minute	1 minute/question
2	20	1 minute	1 minute/question
3	22	1 minute	1 minute/question

You will have to work hard to keep this pace. However, if you work at this rate, you will have extra time to answer questions that are more difficult.

Complete the Answer Sheet as you work. You will not have time to transfer your answers at the end.

Strategies

Matching

DIRECTIONS *Match each definition or date in List A with the related term in List B.*

STRATEGY Scan the reading passage looking for the words, dates, or phrases in List A. Read the sentence where this word or date is found. Is a related term or paraphrase in List B? If not, read the sentence that comes before or after.

TIP The word in List A may be in italics or may be capitalized. The matching word or phrase may be a paraphrase. Be sure to understand the context and don't just match identical words. Sometimes you may use a word from List B more than once.

PRACTICE (answers on page 211)

Paragraph 1

Read the paragraph. Match each item in List A with an item in List B.

English place names are like a record of the history of England. In them we can see vestiges of the languages spoken by the different peoples who have been part of the history of that country. For example, the place name Derby comes from two old Viking words: *deor* (deer) and *by* (small rural settlement). The ending "by" shows up in many English place names. Whitby, Selby, and Enderby are a few examples. "Chester," another common place name ending, is of Saxon origin, and is also seen in the forms "Cester" and "Caster." It refers to a place where Roman soldiers established their forts. Lancaster, for example, means "Fort on the River Lune." Winchester and Dorchester are other examples of place names with this ending. There are even a few traces of the old Celtic language left on the land. The Avon river gets its name from the Celtic word that means just that—"river." As you can see, a simple study of the names of the places on a map can reveal much about the people who named the places.

List A Place name	List B Meaning
1 by	A fort
2 Caster	B deer
3 Avon	C land
	D village
	E river

Reading Tip

Scan for the key word *by*. The reference is *small rural settlement.* The paraphrase for a *small rural settlement* is *village*.
Scan for the key word *Caster*. The reference is *forts* in the next sentence.
Scan for the key word *Avon*. The reference is *river* in the same sentence.

Paragraph 2

Read the paragraph. Match each item in List A with an item in List B.

Although it may seem overwhelming at first, learning to identify wild flowers is not necessarily complicated. The easy way to start is by learning the common characteristics of the different plant families. Members of the mint family are easily recognizable by the four-sided shape of their stems. Mints also have opposite leaves and tubular-lipped flowers. Plants of the carrot family bloom in compound umbels—umbrella-shaped clusters. They are also characterized by hollow flower stalks. Members of the rose family include much more than the familiar garden rose. Apples, strawberries, and raspberries, for example, are all members of the rose family. Plants in this family have opposite leaves, flowers with five petals, and their stems may or may not be thorny.

List A	**List B**
Plant Family	**Characteristic**
4 mint	**A** round flower stalks
5 carrot	**B** square stems
6 rose	**C** alternate leaves
	D flowers in clusters
	E five-petaled blossoms

Paragraph 3

Read the paragraph. Match each item in List A with an item in List B.

Words for different types of traditional Native American shelters are well known in our language, but there is often confusion or misinformation about what type of shelters these words actually refer to. The word *wigwam* refers to a type of shelter that was typical in the northeastern part of what is now the United States. It was a small, dome-shaped dwelling made of a frame of arched poles covered with materials such as grass, brush, reeds, or bark. The *tipi* was typical on the Great Plains. It was a tall, tent-like structure made of the hides of bison stretched over a framework of poles lashed together at the top. Perhaps the most misunderstood word of all is *igloo.* This does not necessarily refer to a house made of snow, although it often does. Among the Inuit, the native people of northern Alaska and Canada, the word simply means *house* and can refer to any dwelling at all: a sod house, a wood shack, a modern house made of concrete, or any other building that people live in.

List A	**List B**
Shelter	**Description**
7 wigwam	**A** a tall tent covered with animal skins
8 tipi	**B** a concrete building
9 igloo	**C** Inuit word for any type of house
	D small, round, covered with plant material
	E a log cabin

Short Answer

DIRECTIONS *Answer the questions below.*
*Write **NO MORE THAN THREE WORDS** for each answer.*
Write your answers in boxes 1 to 3 on your Answer Sheet.

STRATEGY Scan the passage looking for key words found in the question and read for the answer to *who, what, when, where, or how long.*

TIP Do not write more than the suggested numbers of words. If the directions say ***"NO MORE THAN THREE WORDS"*** write ONLY three words or less. DO NOT WRITE FOUR WORDS. You will be penalized.

The *Wh-* word at the beginning of the question tells you what type of specific detail to look for. If you see the question word *who,* you will listen for a name or an occupation. You will listen to something that refers to a person. Study the following lists to learn what to look for.

First word	Look for...
Who	person
What	place, object, emotion
When	time
Where	location
Why	reason
Which	place, person, object
How many	quantity
How long	time, distance

PRACTICE (answers on page 211)

*Read the paragraphs and answer the questions. Write **NO MORE THAN THREE WORDS** for each answer.*

Paragraph 1

A marathon is a type of running race. Its name comes from a legend about the Persian-Greek war. According to the story, a soldier named Phidippides ran from the battlefield in Marathon to Athens, a distance of approximately 26 miles, to carry news about victory. When the first modern Olympics were held in Athens in 1896, the idea of the marathon running race was brought up as a means of popularizing the event. At those games, the marathon was just under 25 miles. In 1908 at the London Olympics, the length of the marathon was changed to 26 miles. At the Paris Olympics in 1924 the official length of the marathon was finally established at 26.2 miles, and that is as it remains to this day.

1 How long is a marathon race now? ....

2 What two places did Phidippides run between? ....

3 Where were the Olympics held in 1908? ....

Paragraph 2

The answer to the question, "Which was the first novel written in English?" depends on how one defines the term "novel." There are a number of works that have tried to claim this honor. Probably the earliest is *Le Morte d'Arthur*, written by Thomas Malory, published in 1485. However, many do not count this as a novel since it is not an original story but a retelling of legends. John Bunyan's 1678 work *Pilgrim's Progress* is another claimant to the title, but because it is allegorical in nature, it also doesn't fit most definitions of "novel." *Pamela*, written by Samuel Richardson in 1740, is widely considered to be the first English language novel. It is written in the form of letters between the characters, as many early novels were.

4 Who wrote *Le Morte d'Arthur*? ....

5 Why isn't *Pilgrim's Progress* considered to be a novel? ....

6 Which novel is generally accepted to be the first English novel? ....

Paragraph 3

The word penguin often brings to mind playful black and white animals sliding on the ice. However, not all of the seventeen species of penguin live in icy parts of the world. In fact, some live in areas where it is quite warm. The Galapagos penguin, for example, lives near the equator. Four penguin species live in the region of Antarctica. The rest are distributed around different areas of the world, in cold, temperate, or tropical zones, but all in the southern hemisphere. There are no native penguins in the northern hemisphere. Penguins live off seafood—shrimp, krill, squid, and different kinds of fish, depending on the species of penguin.

7 How many species of penguin are there in the world? ....

8 Where do all penguins live? ....

9 What do penguins eat? ....

True, False, Not Given and Yes, No, Not Given

These two question types are very similar to each other. The True/False question is concerned with facts in a passage; the Yes/No question is concerned with an author's opinion or attitude.

STRATEGY	Scan the passage for words that match the key words in the statement. The statements may be paraphrases of similar statements in the passage. If there is no similar statement in the passage, the answer is NOT GIVEN.
TIP	Pay attention to adjectives and adverbs (modifiers). A modifier in a question may be the opposite of the modifier in the passage.

DIRECTIONS *Do the following statements agree with the information given in the passage? In Boxes 1–4 on your Answer Sheet write*

TRUE *if the statement agrees with the information in the passage*

FALSE *if the statement contradicts the information in the passage*

NOT GIVEN *if there is no information about this in the passage*

DIRECTIONS *Do the following statements agree with the views of the writer in the passage? In Boxes 1–4 on your Answer Sheet write*

YES *if the statement agrees with the views of the writer*

NO *if the statement contradicts the views of the writer*

NOT GIVEN *if it is impossible to say what the writer thinks about this*

PRACTICE 1 (answers on page 212)

True/False/Not Given

Read the paragraphs and write TRUE, FALSE, or NOT GIVEN next to each statement that follows. For each statement, underline the sentence or sentences in the paragraph where you found the answer. If you cannot find a sentence to underline, the answer is NOT GIVEN.

Paragraph 1

Deep in the Guatemalan rainforest lies Tikal, one of the most important archeological sites of the ancient Mayan civilization. The site contains more than 3,000 buildings, constructed between 600 BC and AD 900. The ancient city was an important ceremonial center with temples, palaces, and a central plaza, as well as numerous dwelling places scattered around the area. Much of the site has been excavated and restored, making it a popular attraction for tourists and students of the ancient Maya. However, many structures are still covered under a thick layer of jungle growth and have yet to be excavated. At its height, Tikal was home to a population of about 90,000. Archeologists have excavated the remains of cotton, tobacco, beans, pumpkins, and peppers, as well as tools used to grow these crops, showing that this was an agricultural society.

1 All of the buildings at Tikal have been excavated. ....

2 Tikal was the home of the most important Mayan king. ....

3 The ancient inhabitants of Tikal were farmers. ....

Paragraph 2

The Hawaiian Islands are a chain of volcanic islands stretching along a line of about 1500 miles in the Pacific Ocean. The chain consists of eight major islands, the largest being the island of Hawaii, as well as some 124 smaller islands and islets. The islands were formed by the movement of the Pacific Plate over a volcanic hot spot. In the late eighteenth and early nineteenth centuries, the islands were known to Europeans as the Sandwich Islands. This was the name given to them by Captain Cook when he first visited the area in 1778. He called them this in honor of the fourth Earl of Sandwich, who had provided the financial backing for Cook's expeditions. By the 1840s, the name Sandwich Islands had largely fallen out of use.

4 Several of the volcanoes on the Hawaiian Islands are still active. ....

5 There are a total of eight islands in the Hawaiian Island chain. ....

6 Captain Cook named the islands after his financial backer. ....

PRACTICE 2 (answers on page 212)

Yes/No/Not Given

Read the paragraph and write YES, NO, or NOT GIVEN next to each statement that follows. For each statement, underline the sentence or sentences in the paragraph where you found the answer. If you cannot find a sentence to underline, the answer is NOT GIVEN.

Paragraph 1

The dangers of driving while using a cell phone are hard to ignore. Statistics from 2009 show close to 1,000 people in the United States killed in traffic accidents where use of a cell phone was reported as a factor in the accident. Note that these numbers show only reported information. The number of traffic deaths caused by distracted drivers with cell phones is likely a good deal higher. Statistics also show that it is the 30- to 39-year-old age group that has the highest number of cell phone–related traffic deaths, rather than the under 20 age group, as would be expected. Cell phone use while driving is more common among women than among men and more common in the southern part of the country than in the north.

1 The reported number of traffic accident deaths caused by cell phone use is much lower than the actual number. ....

2 It is generally assumed that drivers under 20 are more often involved in cell-phone related traffic accidents than older drivers are. ....

3 Laws regarding using a cell phone while driving are too strict. ....

Paragraph 2

The Learning Styles Model and the Multiple Intelligences Theory both provide frameworks for teachers working to organize their classrooms and lessons to maximize the learning experience for all their students. Both these approaches recognize that children learn differently, and they can be used effectively together in the classroom. The Learning Styles Model identifies five areas that influence learning: environment, emotions, social, physical, and psychological. It then looks at different factors within these areas. The environment, for example, can affect learning in terms of sound (some children learn better in a quiet environment while others prefer noise), light (some children prefer a brightly lit environment while others feel better in softer light), and other factors. Social influences include such things as whether a child prefers to work alone or with others, with or without the guidance of an adult, with a routine or in a variety of ways.

4 The Learning Styles Model is a more effective tool than the Multiple Intelligences Theory. ....

5 Light and noise levels can affect how children learn. ....

6 Most children prefer to work with adult guidance. ....

Labeling a Diagram

DIRECTIONS *Label the diagram below. Choose **NO MORE THAN TWO WORDS** from the reading passage for each answer. Write your answers in boxes 1–3 on your Answer Sheet.*

STRATEGY Scan the text for key words that indicate location: *next to, above, across, edge, center, beneath*,

Look for words that indicate geometric patterns: *square, rectangle, bisect*. You don't have to write *a*, *and*, or *the*.

TIP Labeling a Diagram questions test your ability to translate words into pictures. When you read, turn words into pictures in your head, then make a simple drawing on paper before you answer the questions.

PRACTICE (answers on page 212)

Read the paragraphs and label the diagrams. Choose NO MORE THAN TWO WORDS from the reading passage for each answer. Write your answers in boxes 1–3 on your Answer Sheet.

Paragraph 1

The art of carpet weaving is an old Persian tradition. The various motifs that make up the carpet designs often have a symbolic meaning. For example, peacocks represent immortality while peonies symbolize power. Persian carpets usually follow one of three layouts. The medallion layout shows a large decoration in the center of the carpet, often with smaller motifs around it, the whole enclosed by a decorative border. This is probably the most common carpet design. The one-sided layout shows the most predominate design element weighted toward one end of the carpet rather than being placed in the center. The all-over layout shows a pattern distributed all over the surface of the carpet.

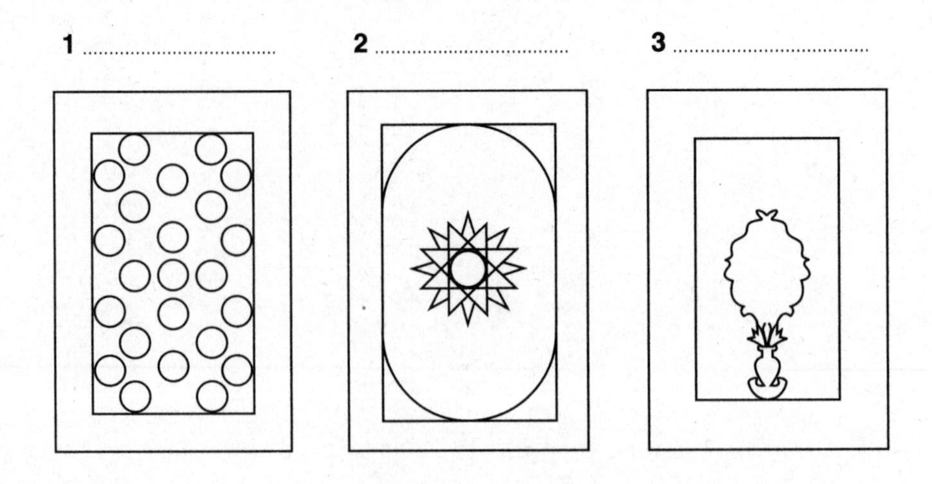

Paragraph 2

The Earth is made up of three main parts: the crust, the mantle, and the core. The crust is the outer layer, and the thinnest. It makes up about 0.5 percent of the Earth's mass and consists of rocks, such as granite and basalt. It is only about 10 kilometers thick under the oceans and about 30 to 50 kilometers thick under the continents. Beneath the crust is the mantle. We know much less about this layer than we know about the crust since we can't see it. It makes up about 50 percent of the Earth's mass. In the Earth's interior, we have the core. This is divided into two parts. The outer core is liquid. It is about 2,100 kilometers thick and makes up about 30 percent of the Earth's mass. The solid inner core is about 1,300 kilometers thick and makes up just 2 percent of the Earth's mass.

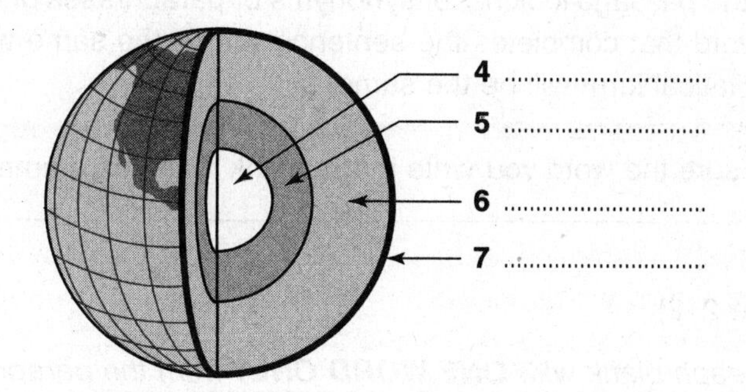

Completing Sentences

DIRECTIONS *Complete the sentences. Choose **ONE WORD ONLY** from the passage for each answer.*

STRATEGY	Try to complete the sentence first, then return to the passage to check your answer. Skim the passage looking for synonyms or paraphrases of words from the sentence. The word that completes the sentence will be the same word in the passage. The grammatical form will be the same.
TIP	Make sure the word you write in the blank matches grammatically.

PRACTICE (answers on page 212)

*Read the paragraph. Fill in each blank with **ONE WORD ONLY** from the paragraph.*

Paragraph 1

The term *insomnia*, from a Latin word meaning *sleepless*, refers to a common sleep disorder where the sufferer has difficulty falling or staying asleep. *Acute insomnia* lasts for just a few days or weeks and is often brought on by a traumatic event, such as job loss or death of a loved one. It happens in situations of temporary stress. *Chronic insomnia* is long term. It is usually defined as insomnia that lasts for a month or longer. Clinical depression, constant stress, and chronic pain are common causes. *Secondary insomnia* is not a disease itself, but is a symptom of some other health condition such as arthritis, cancer, or pain, or it may be caused by a patient's medication. *Primary insomnia*, on the other hand, is a disorder that is not caused by some other medical issue.

1 .... insomnia is a sleep disorder that lasts a short period of time.

2 .... stress is one situation that can lead to chronic insomnia.

3 Secondary insomnia is a sign that the patient has some type of .... problem.

Paragraph 2

Moths and butterflies, animals of the Lepidoptera order, are very similar to each other. However, there are a few characteristics by which you can tell them apart. Generally, butterflies are diurnal, active during the day, and moths are nocturnal, active at night. There are some exceptions to this, though, such as the diurnal buck moth. If you look at a butterfly's antennae, you will notice that they are long and thin with a knob at the end. A moth's antennae, on the other hand, are not thin but feathery. When moths are at rest, they hold their wings out flat, while butterflies at rest hold them up in a vertical position. There are many more species of moths than butterflies. In fact, they make up around 90 percent of the Lepidoptera order.

4 Unlike most other moths, the buck moth is active in the ....

5 Resting butterflies hold their .... vertically.

6 Around 90 percent of Lepidoptera are ....

Paragraph 3

The list of health benefits, both physical and mental, that result from regular exercise is long. Most experts recommend that you get a minimum of thirty minutes of moderate exercise per day, while forty-five minutes or an hour, at least on some days out of every week, is even better. The good news is that you don't have to

Passage 3

Questions 28–40

The Voyages of Christopher Columbus

Christopher Columbus was not alone in his belief that the world was round, but he may have been unique in his determination to open up trade routes to Asia by sailing west. In the 1400s, overland travel from Europe to the gold, silk, and spices of the East was extremely difficult. Political strife, bandits, and harsh desert conditions made most routes practically impassable. Thus arose the motivation of trying to reach that part of the world by sea.

Christopher Columbus, a native of Genoa, Italy, worked for a while as a weaver, his father's trade. He then became a seaman and sailed the Mediterranean. He eventually ended up in Lisbon, Portugal, where his brother worked as a mapmaker, and around 1479, he married a native of that city. Columbus traveled for a time among the Portuguese islands that lay off the west coast of Africa, working as a sugar purchaser. This put him in contact with seamen who talked of islands that they believed lay even further west. Columbus started to dream about sailing west to get to Asia. He tried for years to find financial backing for this journey. At last, the king and queen of Spain agreed to support him in his venture, and he set sail on his first voyage in August of 1492.

In early October, Columbus and his crew landed on a small island in the Bahamas, which Columbus named San Salvador. They explored several more islands in the area, then landed in Cuba on October 28. From there they went on to the island of Hispaniola, landing there in early December. When Columbus returned to Spain in March 1493, he did not bring with him silks and spices from the East. He couldn't report with certainty, either, that he had even found a route to that part of the world, although he believed the islands he had visited might have been off the coast of China or Japan. In any case, he had found new land. The king and queen of Spain rewarded him by appointing him governor general of all the new lands he had found or would find, and he was named Admiral of the Ocean Sea.

Although Columbus had returned from his first trip without the promised cargo of silks and spices, a second voyage was funded. This time he sailed with a fleet of seventeen ships carrying more than one thousand people, who were to establish a Spanish colony. To this end, the ships also carried sheep, pigs, and cattle, the first to be brought to the New World. They left Europe in October of 1493 and landed on the island of Dominica in November. They stayed there briefly, and then went on to visit other islands of the Lesser Antilles before finally landing on Hispaniola. There, Columbus established a colony and served as governor. He also explored other islands of the area, including a return to Cuba and his first visit to Jamaica. He returned to Spain in 1496.

The riches of the East still had not materialized. Nevertheless, in 1498 the king and queen of Spain allowed a third voyage to the New World so that Columbus could carry supplies to the colony on Hispaniola and continue to search for a trade route to the East. This was a trip that was to end in disaster for the explorer. On the last day of July, Columbus and his crew sighted the island of Trinidad for the first time and then spent a couple of weeks exploring the Gulf of Paria, which lies between Trinidad and the coast of South America. They found the mouth of the mighty Orinoco River and realized that this land had to be a continent, not an island. However, they didn't go ashore, but returned to the colony on Hispaniola toward the end of August.

Things were not going well in the colony. The colonists were unruly and, in an attempt to establish order, Columbus had several of them hanged. Needless to say, he was not a popular governor. The Spanish sovereigns had gotten wind of the unrest in the colony and sent Francisco de Bobadilla as their representative to straighten things out. He ended up arresting Columbus and sending him back to Spain in chains. Once back in Spain, Columbus was soon released, but he lost his reputation and several of his honors.

In 1502, Columbus set off on his fourth and final voyage in search of a trade route to the East. During this trip, he explored the coast of Central America for the first time, where he and his crew encountered several native cultures, including some Mayans, and exchanged goods with them. After exploring the area, Columbus and his crew headed back to the colony on Hispaniola. Traveling in ships that had been damaged by storms and termites, they only made it as far as Jamaica before the ships fell apart. There they were forced to stay until they were finally rescued in June of 1504. Columbus returned to Spain never to explore the New World again. He died in 1506.

The history that ensued as a result of Columbus's exploration of the New World has been interpreted from various viewpoints. To some, it meant the introduction of civilization to the New World. Others see it as the beginning of centuries of economic exploitation and oppression. From any viewpoint, however, it cannot be denied that Columbus's travels changed the world.

Complete the notes using words and phrases from the box.

A	funds
B	Lisbon
C	buy sugar
D	sailor
E	mapmaker
F	Genoa
G	publicity
H	riches
I	politics
J	find spices

- Fifteenth-century Europeans wanted to travel to Asia because of the **28** .... there.
- Columbus was born in **29** ....
- After he worked in his father's business, Columbus became a **30** ....
- Columbus traveled to Portuguese islands to **31** ....
- The king and queen of Spain gave Columbus **32** .... for his trip.

Classify the following events as occurring during Columbus's

A first voyage
B second voyage
C third voyage
D fourth voyage

33 European domestic animals were transported to the Americas for the first time.
34 The crew suffered a shipwreck.
35 Columbus's explorations earned him a special title.
36 Columbus executed several men.
37 The crew saw South America for the first time.
38 Columbus discovered Jamaica.
39 Columbus traded with Mayans.
40 Columbus was imprisoned.

IELTS WRITING MODULE

OVERVIEW

In this chapter, you will learn and practice specific strategies based on the two different writing tasks. These strategies will introduce you to the types of topics you will have to address in the writing section. You will learn how to plan, write, and revise your responses to both Task 1 and Task 2. You will review grammar, spelling, and punctuation rules that you will need to know when you write your Task 1 and Task 2 responses. You will also write complete essays in response to sample Task 1 and Task 2 topics.

TASK ONE

GENERAL STRATEGIES

Recognize the Parts of a Graphic
Use the Title

SPECIFIC STRATEGIES

OPENING STATEMENT

State the Purpose
Describe the Graphic Using Time
Describe the Graphic Using Location
Describe a Process Diagram

DESCRIBING DATA

Ask *Wh-* Questions
Show the Steps in a Process

ANALYZING DATA

Compare and Contrast Data
Summarize Similarities and Differences
Describe Changes and Trends
State Facts

GRAMMAR

Prepositions of Time
Prepositions of Amount
Comparisons
Plurals
Articles
Subject–Verb Agreement
Verb Tenses

SPELLING

CHECK AND REVISE

STRATEGY REVIEW

TASK TWO

SPECIFIC STRATEGIES

INTRODUCTION

Restate the Task
Give Your Opinion
Write a Thesis Statement

BODY

Expand Your Thesis Statement
Introduce Details

CONCLUSION

Summarize Your Opinion

GRAMMAR

Gerunds and Infinitives
Modals
Active and Passive Voice
Relative Pronouns—Subject
Relative Pronouns—Object
Real Future Conditionals
Unreal Conditionals

PUNCTUATION

Apostrophes

CHECK AND REVISE

STRATEGY REVIEW

Plan Your Essay
Write Your Essay
Revise Your Essay

Writing Tip

Pay attention to time when you write your responses to the writing tasks. You will have sixty minutes to complete the writing part of the test. You should allow twenty minutes to plan, write, and revise your response to Task 1. You should allow forty minutes to plan, write, and revise your response to Task 2. When you write your responses to the sample topics in this section, divide your time as follows:

Task 1

Part	Number of Words	Planning and Writing Time
Opening statement	15–20	2–3 minutes
Description of details	25–30	4–5 minutes
Description of trends and features	100–120	12–14 minutes

Task 2

Part	Number of Words	Planning and Writing Time
Introduction	25–40	10 minutes
Body	170–200	20 minutes
Conclusion	25–40	5 minutes +5 minutes to review

TASK 1

SAMPLE GRAPHICS

In Task 1, you will see a graphic. A graphic is a drawing. It can be a chart, graph, table, or diagram.

PIE CHART

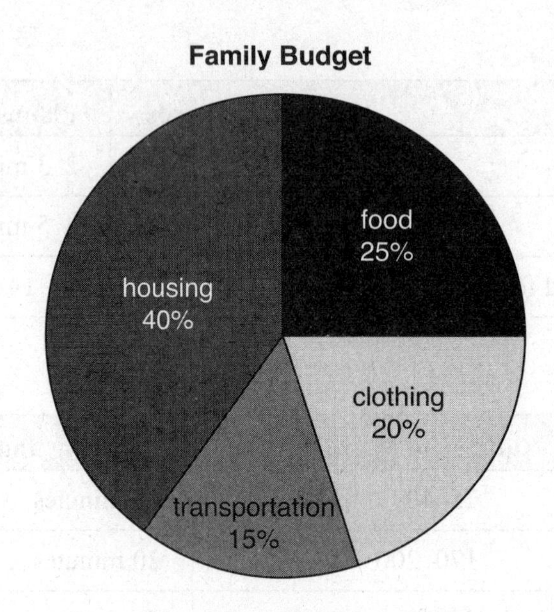

BAR GRAPH

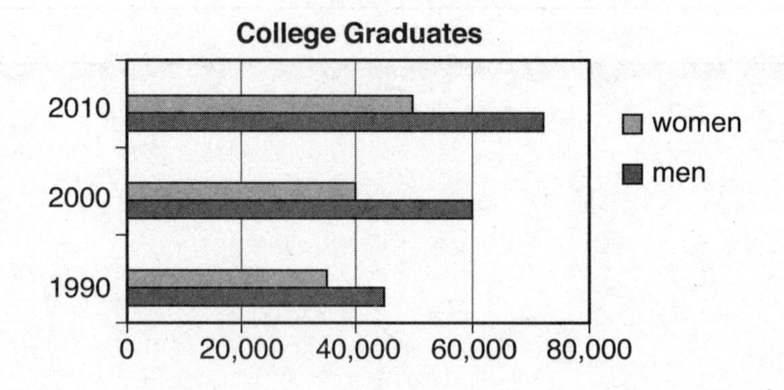

TABLE

New Cars, 2013

Car Model	Miles per Gallon	Base Price
XT3	40	$32,000
AZ9	32	$25,000
RX34	28	$29,000

DIAGRAM

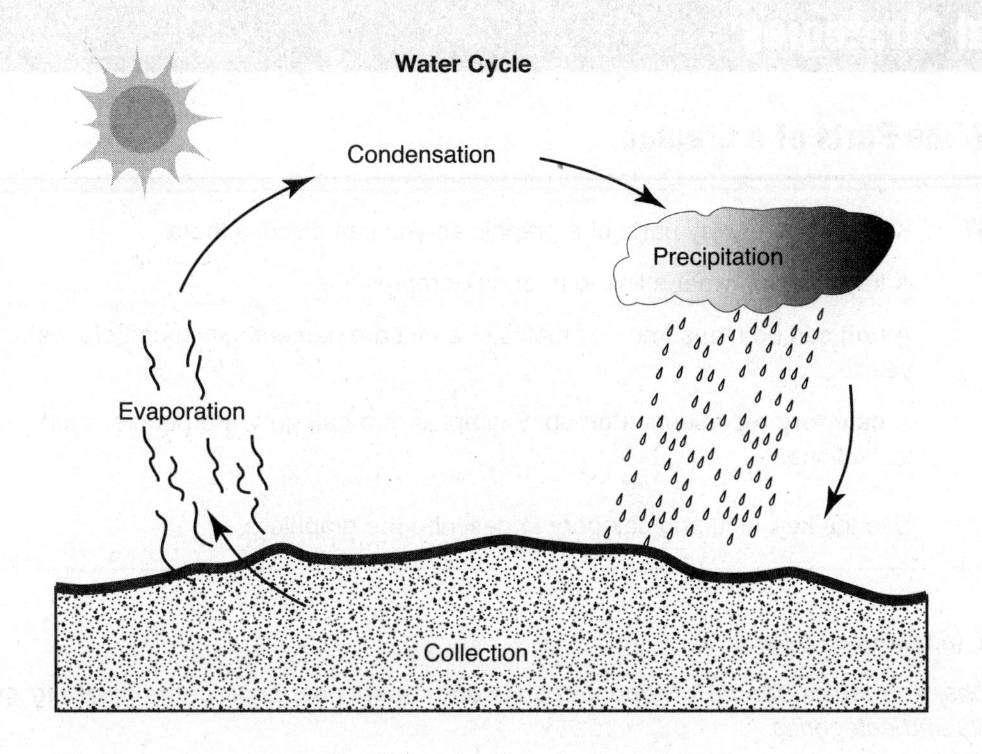

You will have to do one of the following in Task 1:

- Describe and explain the graphic
- Describe a process
- Describe how something works
- Describe an object or
- Describe an event

You will **NOT** give your opinion about the information. You will write a description about what you see. You will have twenty minutes to write 150 words. Judge your time carefully.

General Strategies

Recognize the Parts of a Graphic

STRATEGY Know the three key parts of a graphic so you can discuss them.

A **key** tells you what a line, bar, or color represents.

A **unit** can be measured. Examples of a unit are percentages, numbers, dates, days, or years.

A **category** represents a group. Examples of a category are people, cities, regions, or institutions.

TIP Use the key, unit, and category to describe the graphic.

PRACTICE 1 (answers on page 213)

Charts, graphs, and tables can be divided into units and categories. Look at the following graphics and write the units and categories.

1

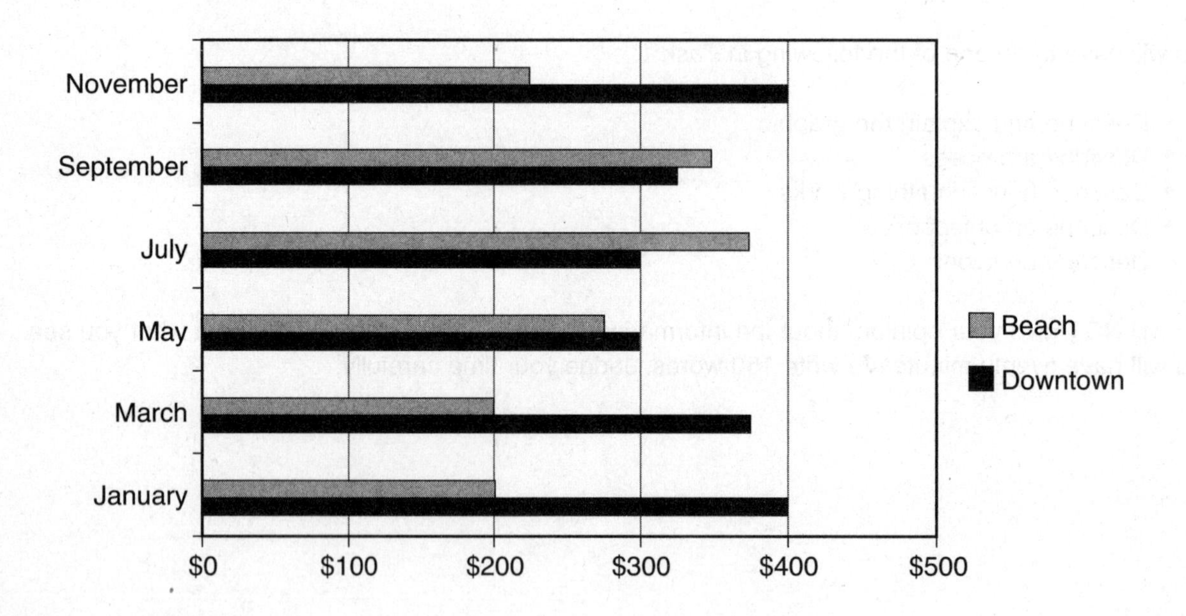

Units: dollars

Categories: months January, March, May, July, September, November

Key: gray—Beach
black—Downtown

2

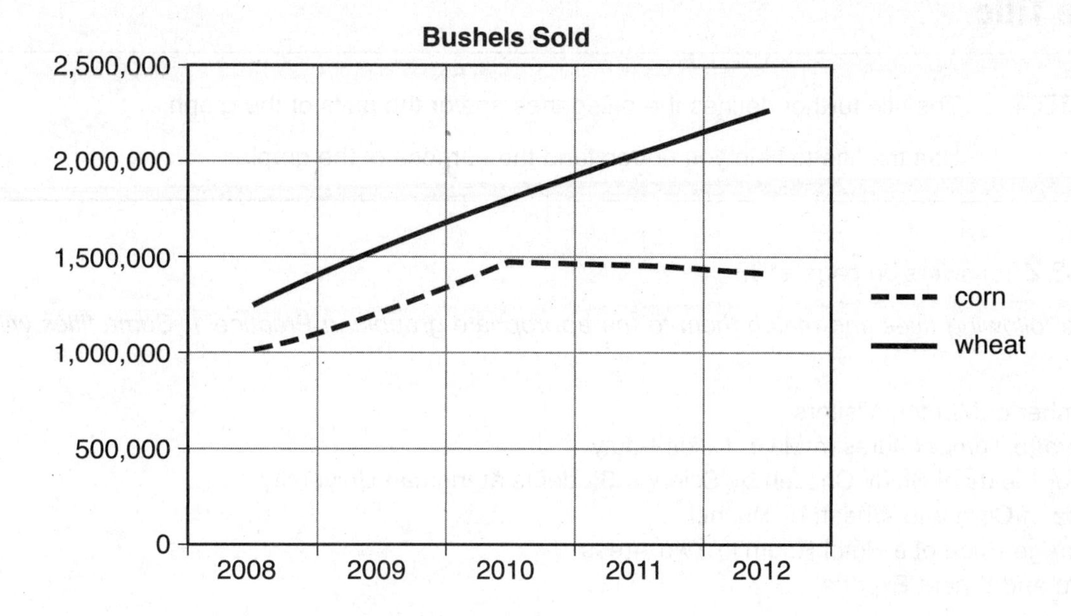

Units: ....

Categories: ....

Key: solid line ....

broken line ....

3

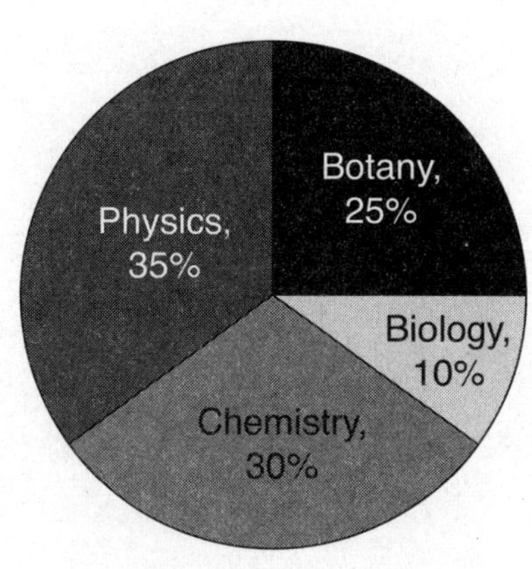

Units: ....

Categories: ....

4

	High	Low
London	73°	60°
Rome	89°	67°
Sydney	60°	45°
Tokyo	82°	66°
Bogota	62°	42°

Units: ....

Categories: ....

Use the Title

STRATEGY	The title further defines the categories and/or the units of the graph.
TIP	Use the title to help you understand the purpose of the graphic.

PRACTICE 2 (answers on page 213)

Read the following titles and match them to the appropriate graphic in Practice 1. Some titles will not be used.

A Number of Monthly Visitors
B Average Temperatures in Major Cities—July
C Major Fields of Study Chosen by Science Students at Ingman University
D Price of Corn and Wheat, by Bushel
E Average Price of a Hotel Room in Two Areas
F Corn and Wheat Exports

Opening Statement

State the Purpose

STRATEGY	In the opening statement, you can describe the graphic by paraphrasing the first sentence of Task 1. The paraphrase will contain specific information that states the specific purpose of the graphic. A general description follows the phrase *gives information about* . . . Change that general description to a specific description. Ask yourself "What?"
TIP	Do NOT repeat the Task exactly as written. Paraphrase or restate the task.

PRACTICE 3 (answers on page 213)

Look at the following charts, graphs, or tables and read the first sentence of the Task. Which statement provides a specific description of the task? Choose the description that most closely matches the chart and that adds more information about the phrase in italics. The first exercise is done for you as a model.

1 The graph below gives information about *computer sales* at the XYZ Company.

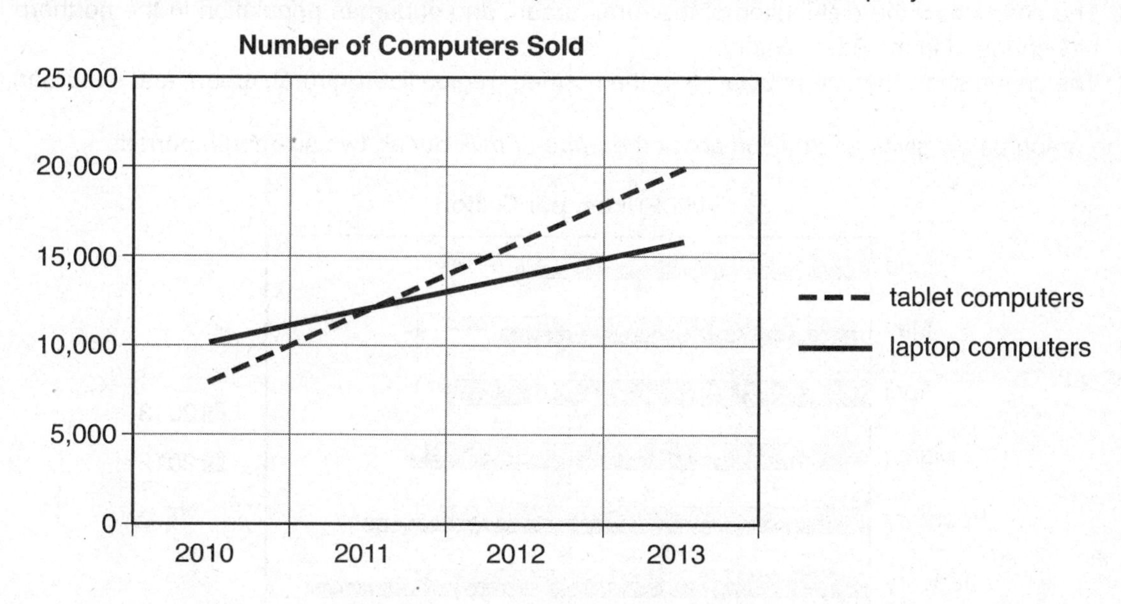

Ask yourself: What? What kind of computers? What about the number of computers sold? Are they increasing? Are they decreasing?

A The graph shows increases in sales of laptop and tablet computers over a four-year period.
B The graph gives information about computer sales at the XYZ Company.
C The graph shows computer sales over time.

Explanation

Statement **A** is a good opening statement. It provides a complete description and it gives specific information about what the graph shows about computer sales. Computer sales are increasing.

Statement **B** is not a good opening statement. It repeats the task exactly as written.
Statement **C** is incomplete. It includes important information, but it doesn't mention what the graph tells us about computer sales.

2 The charts below show *population distribution* in the northern region in two different years.

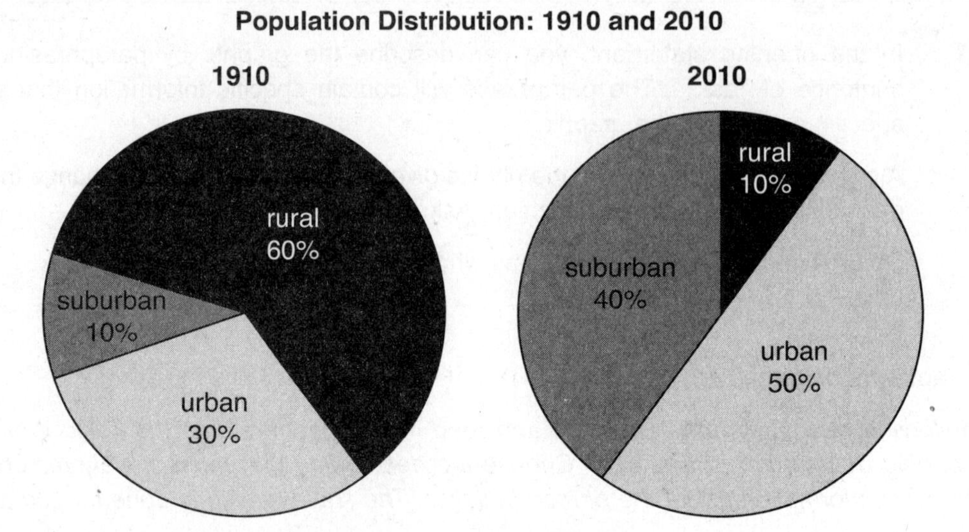

A The charts show where people lived in 1910 and 2010.
B The charts how the distribution of the rural, urban, and suburban population in the northern region has changed in the past century.
C The charts show that the population of the northern region lives in rural, urban, and suburban areas.

3 The graph below gives information about the *price of milk* during two six-month periods.

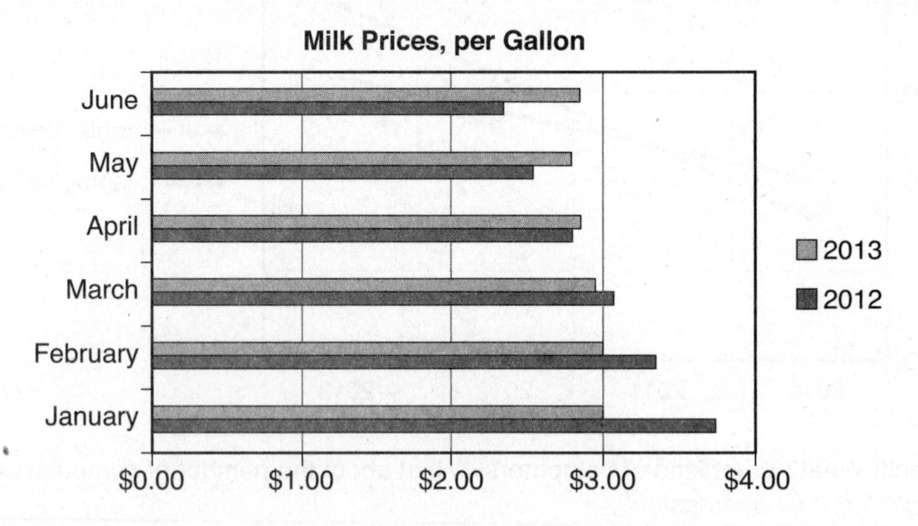

A The graph shows the price of milk at different times.
B The graph compares the average price of a gallon of milk in the first six months of 2012 and 2013.
C The graph shows how much people had to pay for milk recently.

4 The table below shows information about *drivers* and *traffic accidents*.

Drivers Causing Traffic Accidents, by Age

Age Group	15–20yrs	20–30yrs	30–40yrs	40–50yrs	50–60yrs	65+yrs
Percentage of Total Accidents	25%	18%	15%	10%	12%	20%

A The table shows the percentage of traffic accidents caused by drivers in different age groups.
B The table shows that people of different ages cause traffic accidents.
C The table shows how old different drivers are when they have accidents.

Describe the Graphic Using Time

STRATEGY	In the opening statement, add time to the description of the graphic. You can describe the graphic by restating the first sentence of Task 1 and providing more detail. The detail can be time. Time can be hours, days, years, seasons, or historic periods.
TIP	Not all graphs or charts use time. But if time is part of the chart, you should use it in your restatement.

PRACTICE 4 (answers on page 213)

Look at the following charts, graphs, or tables and read the first sentence of the Task. Write a description. Restate the Task and add details about time. The first exercise is done for you as a model.

1 The graph below shows information about museum attendance in two cities *during the year.*

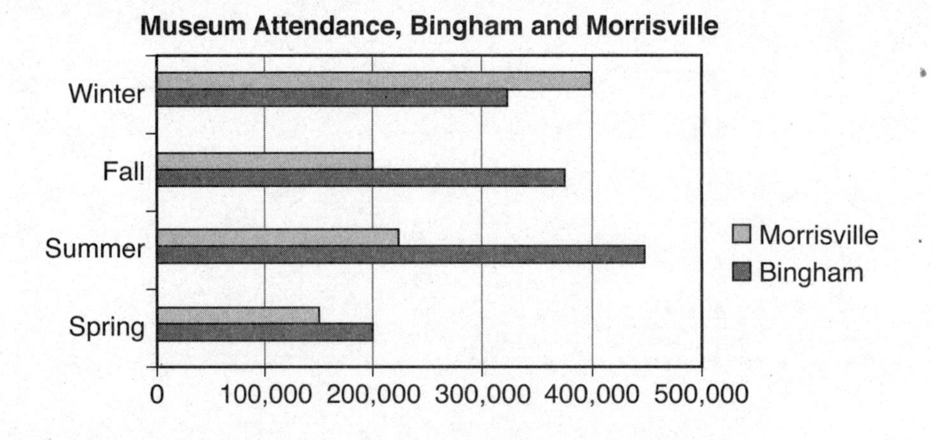

Ask yourself: When? What are the seasons with the greatest attendance?

A The graph shows the number of people who went to museums last year.
B The graph shows how many people attended museums in each of the four seasons of the year in Bingham and Morrisville.
C The graph shows the changes in museum attendance in Bingham and Morrisville

Explanation

Statement **A** is too general. It does not mention the amount of time or the specific cities covered by the chart.
Statement **B** is a good opening statement. It mentions all the important details—what the chart is about, the places, and the periods of time covered.
Statement **C** is incomplete. It does not mention the time frame covered.

2 The graph below shows the numbers of students that enrolled in Brownsville College *in different years*.

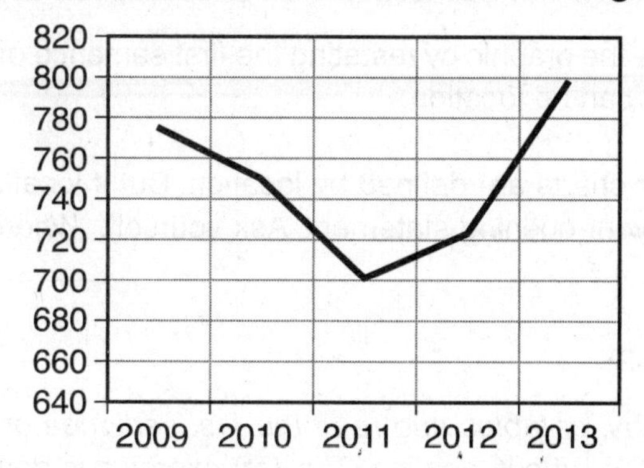

Statement: ....

3 The graph below shows the literacy rates *in the history* of two countries.

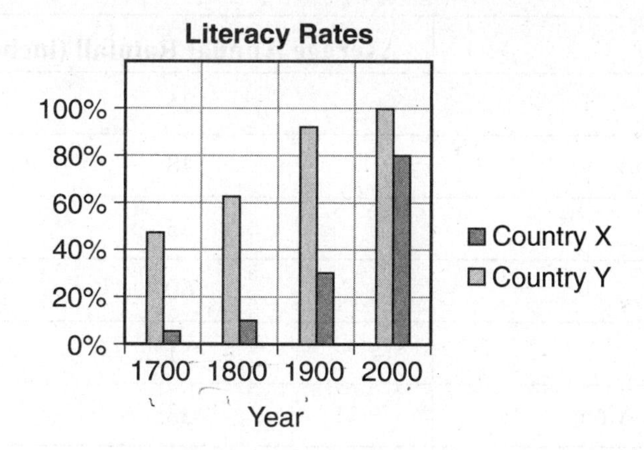

Statement: ....

4 The table below shows the recorded temperature in Oslo, Norway on the *afternoon of August 10*.

Oslo, August 10

Time	Temperature
1:00 PM	21°
2:00 PM	21°
3:00 PM	21°
4:00 PM	20°
5:00 PM	19°
6:00 PM	18°

Statement: ....

Describe the Graphic Using Location

STRATEGY In the opening statement, add location to the description of the graphic.

You can describe the graphic by restating the first sentence of Task 1 and providing more detail. The detail can be location.

TIP Not all graphs or charts are defined by location. But if location is part of the chart, you should use it in your opening statement. Ask yourself: "*Where?*"

PRACTICE 5 (answers on page 213)

Look at the following charts, graphs, or tables and read the first sentence of the Task. Write a description restating the Task and adding details about location. The first exercise is done for you as a model.

1 The table below shows information about rainfall *in several cities.*

Average Rainfall by City

City	Average Annual Rainfall (inches)
Paris	25
New York	48
Caracas	33
Tokyo	60
Cairo	1
Buenos Aires	33
Sydney	40

Where: Cities in different countries; cities around the world
Ask yourself: Where?

A The table shows the average rainfall in several different cities around the world, in inches.
B The table shows how much rain falls on average in different places.
C The table shows the average rainfall in Paris.

Explanation

Statement **A** is a good opening statement. It is a complete description of the content of the table, including a specific description of the places.
Statement **B** is missing a specific description of the places shown on the table.
Statement **C** is incomplete. It only mentions one of the places covered on the table.

PRACTICE 1 (answers on page 214)

Study the graph and the model essay below. Complete the blanks with the prepositions from the box. Some words may not be used. Some may be used more than once.

in	from	between	until	to	since

The graph below gives information about the numbers of annual visitors to the Marine Museum.

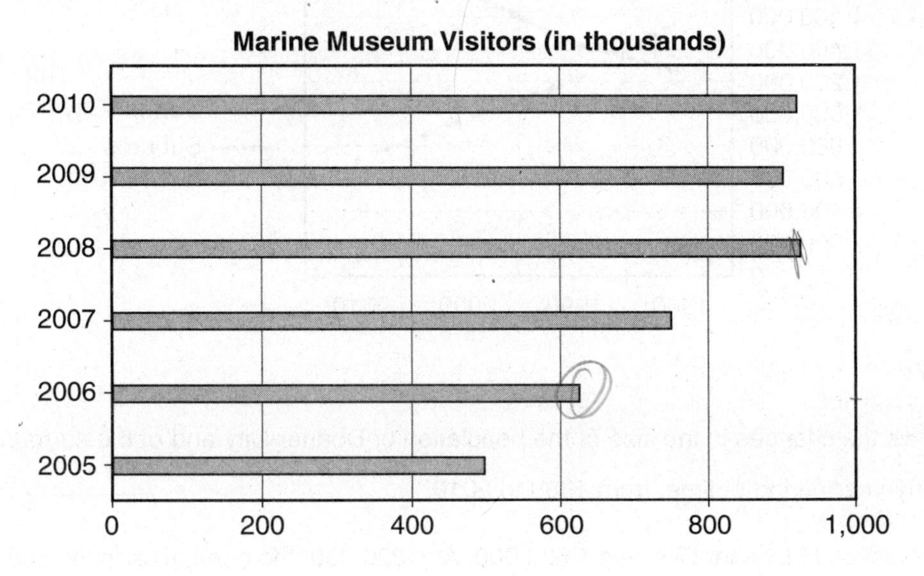

Model Essay

The graph shows the number of people who visited the Marine Museum each year, **1** .... 2005 to 2010. The number of annual visitors increased steadily for several years and then started to level off.

2.............. 2005, there were 500,000 visitors to the museum. The following year, the number rose to a little over 600,000. The number of annual visitors continued to rise **3**.............. 2008, when it reached a little over 900,000.

In 2009, there was a change. **4**.............. this year, the number of visitors fell to exactly 900,000. The next year it rose slightly, but was still a little less than it had been in 2008.

5.............. 2005 and 2008, there were large annual increases in the numbers of annual visitors. The small decrease and increase **6**.............. 2009 and 2010 show a leveling off in the numbers of annual visitors to the Marine Museum.

Prepositions of Amount

We use verbs such as *rise, increase, go up, fall, decrease*, and *go down* to talk about changes in amounts on a chart or graph. We use the prepositions *from, to*, and *by* together with these verbs.

Preposition	Use	Example
from	The starting amount	Prices fell from $200.
to	The ending amount	The number rose to over a million.
by	The amount of the change	The cost increased by 25 percent.

PRACTICE 2 (answers on page 214)

Study the graph and model essay below. Complete the blanks with the prepositions from the chart above.

The graph below gives information about population changes in Donner City and its suburbs.

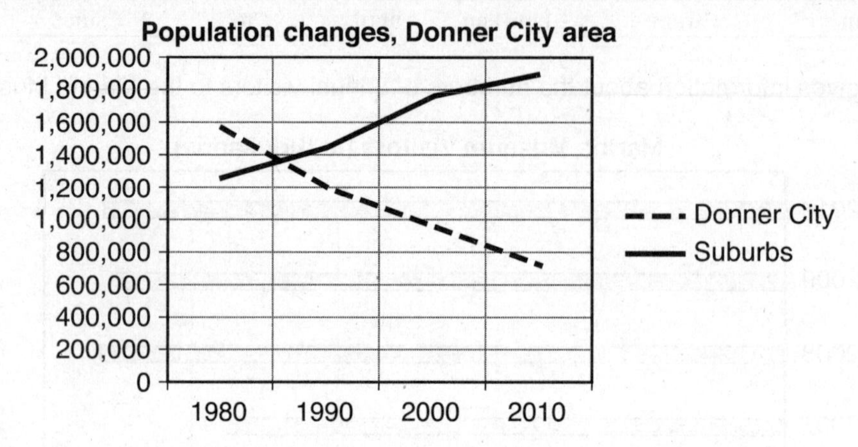

Model Essay

This graph shows the changes in the size of the population of Donner City and of the surrounding suburban area over a thirty-year period of time, from 1980 to 2010.

In 1980, the population of Donner City was 1,600,000. At 1,200,000, the population in the suburbs was lower **1**.............. 400,000. Over the next thirty years, the population of Donner City fell while the population of the suburbs rose. During that time, the Donner City population decreased **2**.............. about 50 percent. In the meantime, the suburban population rose **3**.............. almost 2,000,000.

Between 1980 and 1990, the population of Donner City fell **4**.............. 1,600,000 **5**.............. about 1,200,000. During the same period of time, the population of the suburbs rose **6**.............. 1,200,000 **7**.............. almost 1,600,000. Over the next ten years, the population in the city fell **8**.............. about 200,000 while the suburban population continued to rise and approached 1,800,000.

Overall, this graph shows that the population decreased in the city just as steadily as it increased in the suburbs.

Comparisons

We can compare things in several ways.

More, fewer, less

More indicates a bigger amount.	*More people visited the museum in 2010.*
Fewer and *less* indicate a smaller amount.	
Fewer is used with plural nouns.	*The company sold fewer cars last year.*
Less is used with non-count nouns.	*The company made less money last year.*

Comparative Adjectives

We form a comparative adjective two ways: (1) by adding *-er* to the end of the adjective or (2) by using the word *more* in front of it.

Add *-er* to one syllable adjectives. For words that follow the consonant–vowel–consonant spelling pattern, double the last consonant when adding the *-er* ending.

small → smaller		high → higher
big → bigger	BUT	cheap → cheaper
hot → hotter		cold → colder

Add *-er* to two-syllable adjectives ending in *-y*. Change the *y* to *i*.

busy → busier
rainy → rainier
easy → easier

Use *more* for longer adjectives.

expensive → more expensive
populated → more populated
important → more important

PRACTICE 3 (answers on page 215)

Study the table and the model answer below. Complete the blanks with comparative words from the box. Some words may not be used. Some may be used more than once.

more	higher	fewer	cheaper
less	lower	busier	

The table below gives information about the average number of servings of ice cream sold each day in two different years.

Springer's Café Ice Cream Sales

	April	May	June	July	August	September
2011	15	25	50	55	60	25
2012	25	35	65	80	75	30

The table shows the average number of ice cream servings sold daily for the months of April through September during the years 2011–2012.

Model Essay

The café was **1**............... in 2012 than in 2011. Looking month by month, the average number of servings sold was **2**............... in 2012. For example, in April of 2011, there was an average of 15 servings sold daily, while in April of 2012 the average was 25. In each of the months shown, the average number of servings sold daily is **3**.............. for 2011 than it is for the corresponding months in 2012.

In 2011, **4**.............. servings were sold in August than in any other month. In 2012, **5**.............. servings were sold in July than in any other month. In both years, **6**.............. servings were sold in April than in any other month.

Overall the table shows **7**.............. sales in 2012 than in 2011. It also shows a significantly **8**.............. number of sales in June, July, and August than in the other months.

Plurals

Count nouns are either singular or plural. A singular noun refers to one thing. A plural noun refers to more than one thing.

Most nouns form the plural by adding *–s*:

year → years
product → products
price → prices

Nouns that end in *-s, -z, -ch*, and *-sh* form the plural by adding *-es*:

watch → watches
crash → crashes

Nouns that end in a consonant + *y* have a spelling change–change the *y* to *ie*, then add *-s*:

family → families
dictionary → dictionaries

Some plural forms are irregular, for example:

man → men
woman → women
person → people
child → children

PRACTICE 4 (answers on page 215)

Study the graph and the model essay below. Complete the blanks with words from the box, changing them to the plural form where necessary. All the words will be used more than once.

man	doctor	year
woman	salary	rate

The graph below gives information about new doctors' salaries.

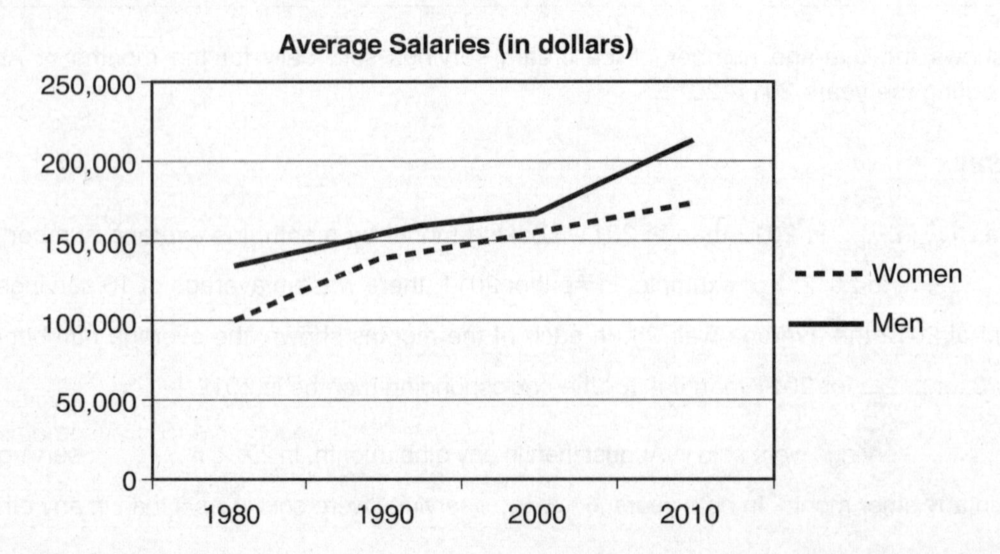

Model Essay

The chart compares the average **1**.............. of men and women who have just become **2**.............. over a period of thirty **3**.............., from 1980 to 2010. Women's salaries remained lower than men's throughout the entire period.

In 1980, the average **4**.............. of a **5**.............. just starting out her career as a **6**.............. was $100,000. During that same year, the average salary of a **7**.............. in the same situation was a little under $150,000. During the next ten **8**.............., women's salaries increased at a faster **9**.............. than men's. In 1990, a woman earned an average salary of just under $150,000 while a man earned a little over that same amount.

The **10**.............. of both men and **11**.............. continued to increase at a similar rate over the next ten years. Then, between 2000 and 2010, the salaries of **12**.............. started increasing at a faster **13**.............. . By 2010, **14**.............. were earning over $200,000 a year on average, while **15**.............. were earning a good deal less than that.

Articles

All singular nouns must be preceded by a determiner. A determiner can be an article: *a/an* or *the*.

A/an

A/an are indefinite articles. They do not refer to any definite or specific item. *A* is used with nouns that begin with consonants. *An* is used with nouns that begin with vowels.

To make concrete, you need a machine to mix sand and water.	This sentence does not refer to any specific machine. It could be any concrete-mixing machine.
Eating an apple every day will improve your health.	You do not need to eat a particular apple to improve your health. Any apple will do.

The

The is a definite article. It refers to something specific. It can precede singular, plural, and non-count nouns.

The sun shines 360 days a year in Arizona.	There is only one *sun* in existence that shines in Arizona.
The teacher gave us some homework.	Both speaker and audience know the reference.
The rooms in this hotel cost less on weekends.	A phrase in the sentence defines the noun.
A machine mixes sand and water to make concrete. The machine can hold up to 250 gallons of concrete.	Use *the* in the second mention of something in the paragraph or text.
(A) Hotels often charge less on weekends. *(B) Rain falls less frequently over desert areas.*	When a plural or non-count noun is indefinite, an article is not required.

PRACTICE 5 (answers on page 215)

Study the diagram and the excerpt from a model essay below. Complete the blanks with a, an, the, *or* ∅ *(to indicate no article is needed). Remember, the first mention of an object in the text is considered indefinite.*

The diagram below shows the steps and equipment involved in recycling paper.

Paper Recycling

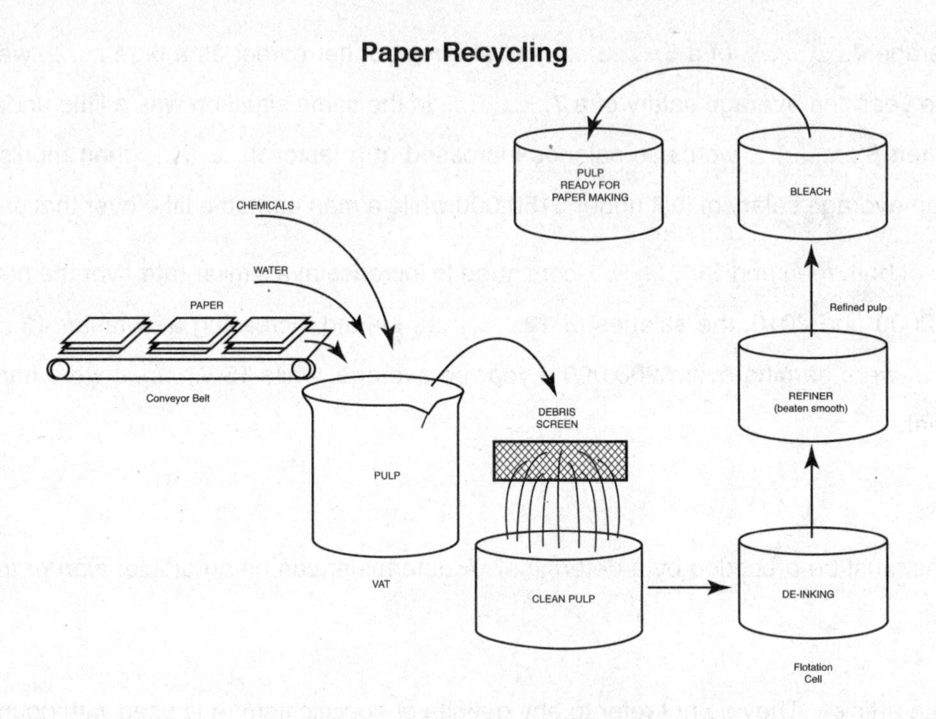

Model Essay

1.............. bales of **2**.............. paper move up **3**.............. conveyer belt. They enter **4**.............. vat. There, **5**.............. paper is mixed with **6**.............. water and **7**.............. chemicals to form **8**.............. pulp. Next, **9**.............. pulp goes through **10**.............. screen. **11**.............. screen removes debris from **12**.............. pulp.

Subject–Verb Agreement

The main verb must agree with the subject of the sentence or clause. If the subject is singular, the verb is singular. If the subject is plural, the verb is plural.

The graph shows the cost of different clothing items. (singular subject, singular verb)

The graphs show the cost of different clothing items. (plural subject, plural verb)

Non-count nouns always take a singular verb.

Milk costs more in the winter. (non-count noun, singular verb)

Know the subject of your sentence. Sometimes there might be a phrase or clause between the subject and the verb.

The computers sold by that company are more expensive. (plural subject, plural verb)

Some nouns look plural but are actually singular. Nouns that end with *-ics* are singular (*mathematics, politics, athletics*). The names of diseases are singular (*mumps, measles*). The noun *news* is singular.

Mathematics was the most popular school subject last semester. (singular subject, singular verb)

The names of companies are singular, even if they include plural words.

Intelligent Systems sells more computers than its competitors. (singular subject, singular verb)

Sums of money take singular verbs.

Five hundred dollars isn't a very large sum of money. (singular subject, singular verb)

Words that begin with *every* and *no* (everybody, everything, nobody, nothing) take singular verbs.

Everyone rides the bus for free after midnight. (singular subject, singular verb)

PRACTICE 6 (answers on page 215)

Study the chart and the model essay below. Complete the blanks with the verbs in parentheses. Choose the verb that agrees with the subject.

The chart below presents the breakdown of professional time for elementary school teachers in the Wardsville school district.

Professional Time: Elementary School Teachers

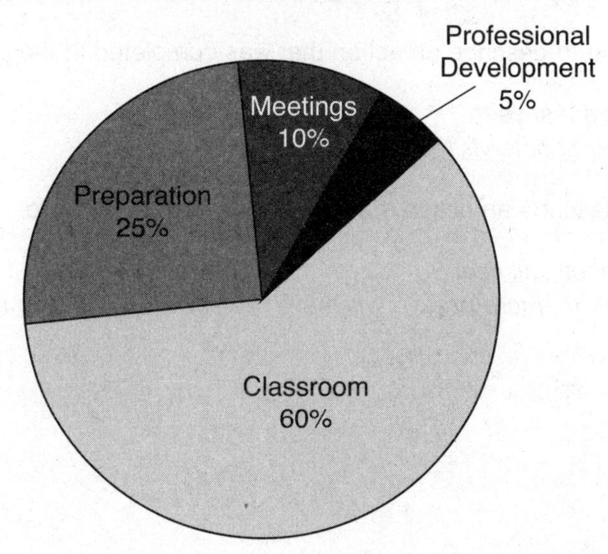

Model Essay

The chart **1**.............. (show/shows) how elementary school teachers in the Wardsville school district **2**.............. (spend/spends) their professional time. Teachers working in elementary school **3**.............. (spend/spends) the largest portion of their time in the classroom. Professional development activities, on the other hand, **4**.............. (take/takes) up the least amount of teachers' time.

An elementary school teacher in Wardsville **5**.............. (spend/spends) a little over half of his or her professional time—60 percent of it—in the classroom. The rest of the time **6**.............. (are/is) taken up with activities such as preparation, meetings, and professional development activities. Preparation **7**.............. (take/takes) up one-fourth of a teacher's professional time. Meetings **8**.............. (take/takes) up 10 percent of it. Professional development activities **9**.............. (account/accounts) for just 5 percent of a teacher's time.

Overall, the chart **10**.............. (show/shows) that teachers **11**.............. (spend/spends) a significant portion of their professional time outside of the classroom. Forty percent of their time—close to half of it—**12**.............. (are/is) spent in other types of activities.

Verb Tenses

You can use a few simple verb tenses to describe the graphics in Writing Task 1.

Use the **simple present tense** to refer to an action or state that is always true.

> *The graph shows information about consumer spending in the past decade.*
> *Houses cost more in Paris than in Bogota.*

Use the **present perfect tense** to refer to an action that started in the past and continues to the present.

> *Prices have increased more than fifty percent since 2005.*
> *The number of annual visitors has fallen since they closed part of the museum.*

Use the **simple past tense** to describe an action that was completed in the past.

> *Prices increased last year.*
> *Over one million people visited the museum in 2009.*

Use the **future tense** to describe an action that will take place in the future.

> *Next month, prices will rise.*
> *In the next decade, more people will leave the suburbs to live in the city.*

PRACTICE 7 (answers on page 215)

Study the model essay below. Complete the blanks with the correct form of the verb in parentheses.

The charts below show the allocation of funds in the town budget of Greensboro.

Town Budget for Greensboro

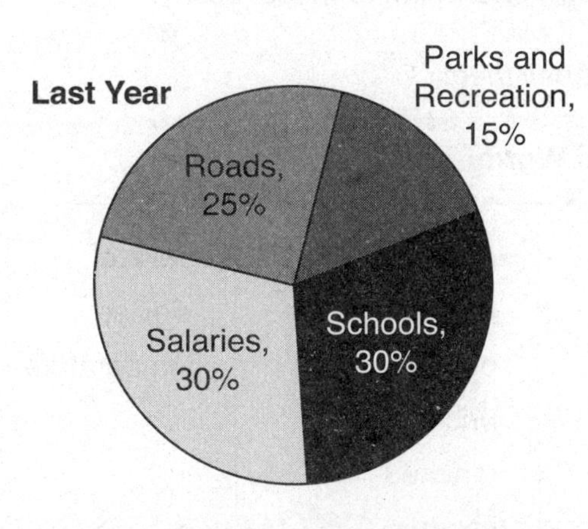

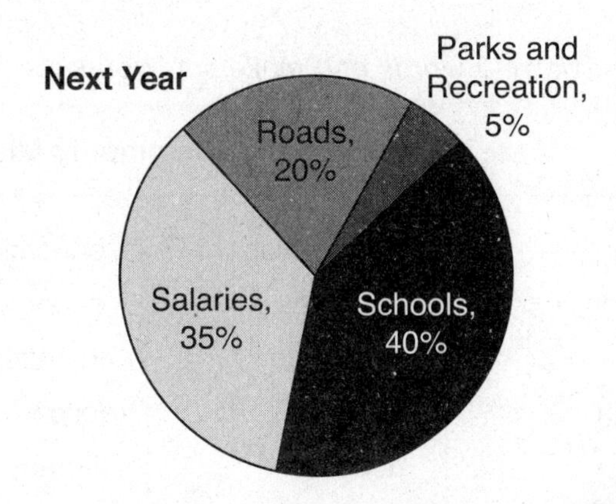

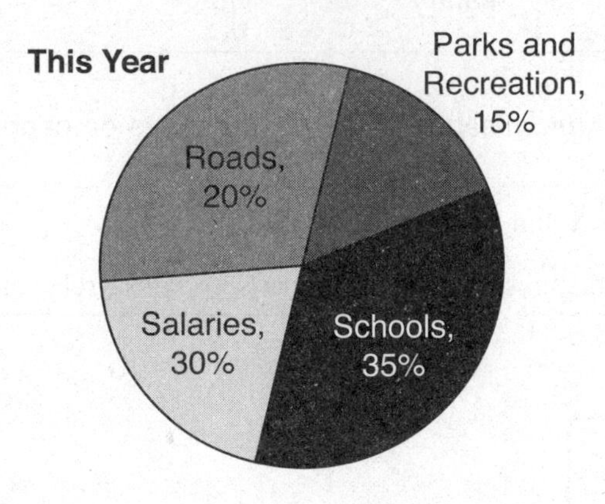

Model Essay

The charts compare the budget of the town of Greensboro in three different years. Last year, the town **1**.............. (spend) an equal portion of its budget on schools and salaries. Thirty percent of the budget **2**.............. (go) to each of those areas. Spending on roads **3**.............. (take) up another 25 percent of the budget, while the smallest amount—15 percent—**4**.............. (go) to parks and recreation.

This year, spending on schools **5**.............. (increase) 5 percent since last year. Spending on schools **6**.............. (remain) the same since last year, while spending on roads **7**.............. (decrease) 5 percent.

Next year, the town **8**.............. (spend) an even greater portion of its budget on schools—40 percent. Spending on salaries **9**.............. (rise) to 35 percent. Spending on roads **10**.............. (stay) the same, at 20 percent. Spending on parks and recreation **11**.............. (drop) to 5 percent.

The town always **12**.............. (spend) more on schools than it does on roads.

Spelling

This section presents some words that are often misspelled by IELTS test takers. This section also has a model essay for Task 1. See how the strategies you learned are shown in the model essay.

Study the following words and make sure you know how to spell them.

Commonly Misspelled Words

almost	comparison	education	occurred	several
although	countries	enough	percentage	similar
before	difference	increased	population	temperature
children	different	follow	price	
career	doubled	literacy	reached	
compared	dramatically	occur	salary	

Study the following task and model essay. Find and correct the misspelled words. (answers on page 215)

> The graph below shows literacy rates through history in Country X and Country Y.
>
> Summarize the information by selecting and reporting the main features, and make comparisons where relevant.

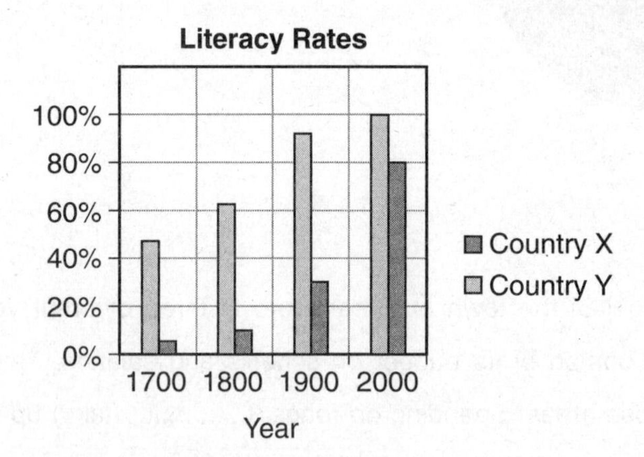

The graph gives information about litracy rates in two countrys over a period of sevral centuries, from 1700 until 2000. While the literacy rates in both countrys incresed in each century, the rates in Country X remained higher than in Country Y in every year shown.

In 1700, more than 40 percent of the popalation in Country X was literate. In Country Y, however, a much smaller percenage of the people could read. In fact, the litracy rate was amost zero. Allthough the number of people who could read grew in both contrys over the next centuries, the litrcy rate in Country Y remained low. By 1900 only about 30 percent of the people in that country could read, while the litrcy rate in Country X in the same year was well over 80 percent.

By 2000, the last year shown on the graph, 100 percent of the people in Country X could read. The litrcy rate in Country Y had reeched 80 percent, but this was still low as compard with Country X.

Check and Revise

(answers on page 216)

As you write your response, ask yourself these questions.

OPENING STATEMENT

- ❑ Did I paraphrase the task?
- ❑ Did I make it more specific?
- ❑ Did I add time and/or location?

DESCRIBING DATA

- ❑ Did I select the important data and features?

ANALYZING DATA

- ❑ Did I interpret the data without giving opinions?

LENGTH

- ❑ Did I write at least 150 words?

PRACTICE

Read the following tasks and responses. Use the checklist above to determine if the writer completed the task. Write an analysis of the response where your answer is "NO." The first task is done for you as an example.

1

The graph below gives information about new doctor's salaries.
Summarize the information by selecting and reporting the main features, and make comparisons where relevant.

Write at least 150 words.

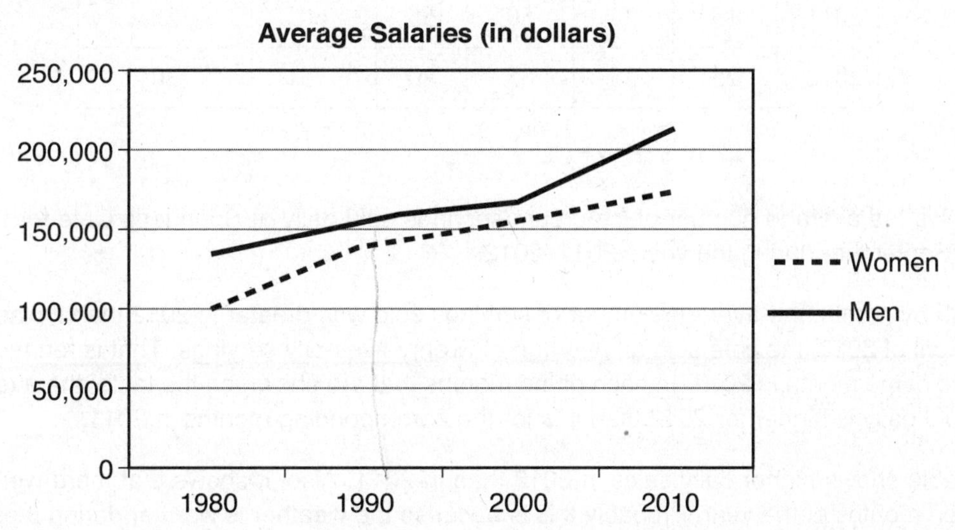

Response

The chart shows how much money new doctors earned each year. It shows that men earned more money than women every year.

In 1980, a new woman doctor earned an average salary of $100,000, while the average salary of a man who was a new doctor was almost $150,000. In the next decade, women's salaries increased more quickly than men's. In 1990, a woman earned an average salary of close to $150,000, while a man earned a little more than that, so their salaries were almost equal.

Both men's and women's salaries continued growing. However, between 2000 and 2010, men's salaries started growing more rapidly. In 2010, a man's average salary was more than $200,000. A woman's was around $175,000.

Analysis

The opening statement is incomplete. It doesn't mention the time frame covered by the graph or the detail that the information relates to *new* doctors.

Important information about overall trends and details are included. Comparisons of men's and women's salaries and their different rates of growth are described although some information is missing, for example: How did trends change between 1990 and 2000? Only facts and no opinions are included.

At 120 words, this response is 30 words too short.

2

> The table below gives information about the average number of servings of ice cream sold each day in two different years.
> Summarize the information by selecting and reporting the main features, and make comparisons where relevant.

Write at least 150 words.

Springer's Café Ice Cream Sales

	April	May	June	July	August	September
2011	15	25	50	55	60	25
2012	25	35	65	80	75	30

Response

The table shows the average number of ice cream servings sold daily at Springer's Café for the months of April through September during the years 2011–2012.

Looking month by month, the average number of servings sold was greater in 2012 than it was in 2011. For example, in April of 2012, the café sold an average of twenty-five daily servings. That is ten more than were sold during the same month in 2011. In each of the months that are shown on the table, the average number of servings sold daily is higher for 2012 than it is for the corresponding months in 2011.

Overall, the table shows higher daily sales in 2012 than in 2011. Also, it shows that there were more sales made in certain months of the year. Probably this is because the weather is warmer during those months so more people want ice cream then.

3

The chart below presents the break down of professional time for elementary school teachers in the Wardsville school district.

Summarize the information by selecting and reporting the main features, and make comparisons where relevant.

Write at least 150 words.

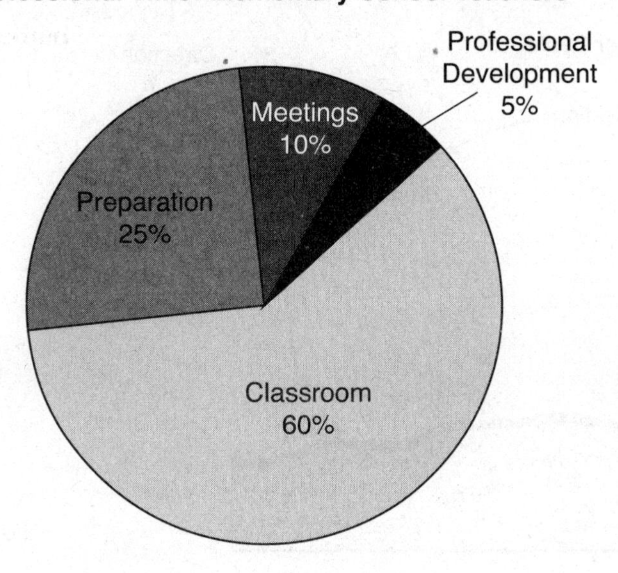

Response

The chart shows how elementary school teachers spend their professional time. These teachers spend the greatest percentage of their professional time in the classroom. On the other hand, they spend the smallest amount of their time participating in professional development activities.

Elementary school teachers spend a little more than half their time (60 percent of it) in the classroom. The rest of their professional time is spent participating in activities such as preparation, meetings, and professional development activities. Twenty-five percent of their time is spent in preparation, ten percent is spent in meetings, and just five percent of their professional time is spent in professional development activities.

What this chart shows is that teachers spend a lot of time involved in activities outside the classroom. I was surprised by this because I think teachers should spend most of their time in class with their students. But these teachers spend almost half their time in other types of activities.

4

The diagrams below show the process of hurricane formation and the hurricane's structure.

Summarize the information by selecting and reporting the main features, and make comparisons where relevant.

Write at least 150 words.

Formation of a Hurricane

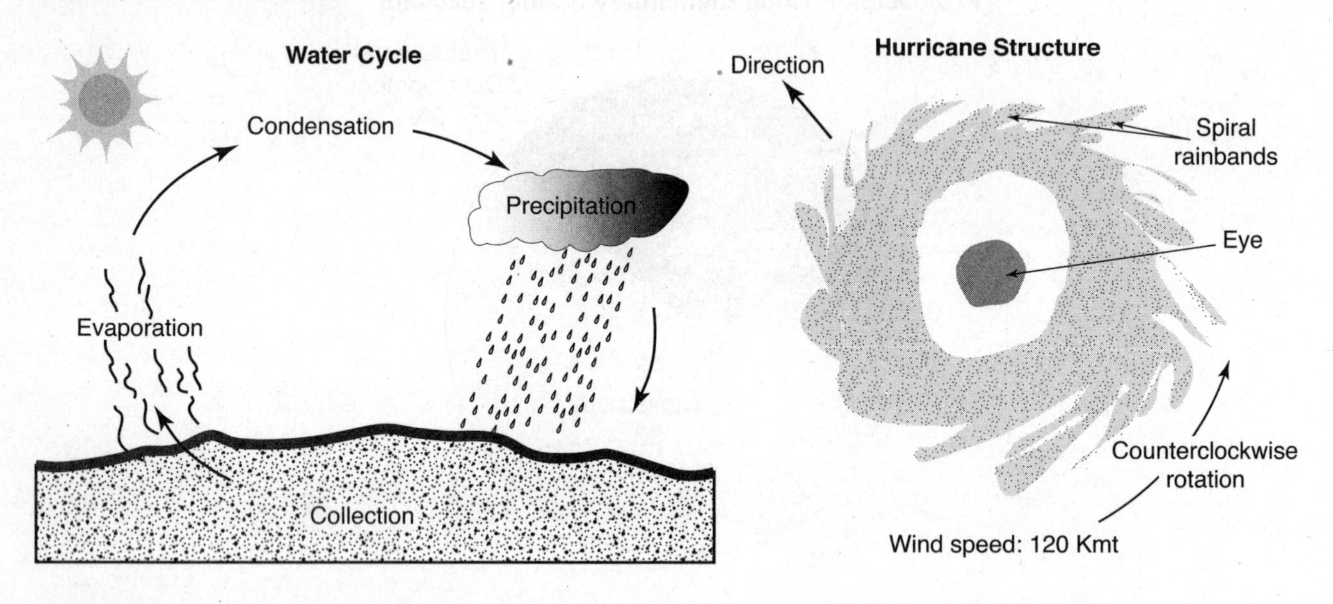

Response

The diagrams show the process that occurs when a hurricane forms and the structure of the hurricane after it forms. This process takes place over the ocean. A hurricane begins to form when humid air moves over the warm ocean. When this happens, water evaporates from the ocean and rises into the air. As it evaporates and rises, it becomes cool and condenses. The condensation of the rising air releases heat, and this causes the air to become lighter and to rise more. Then, wind is created as the rising air pulls moisture from the ocean. The hurricane forms in a spiral shape, with an eye at the center. Rain bands rotate around the eye as the entire hurricane moves forward.

STRATEGY REVIEW

(answers on page 216)

Read and respond to the following tasks. You should spend about 20 minutes on each task.

1

> The charts below show the native languages spoken by students at Roslindale High School in two different years.
>
> Summarize the information by selecting and reporting the main features, and make comparisons where relevant.

Write at least 150 words.

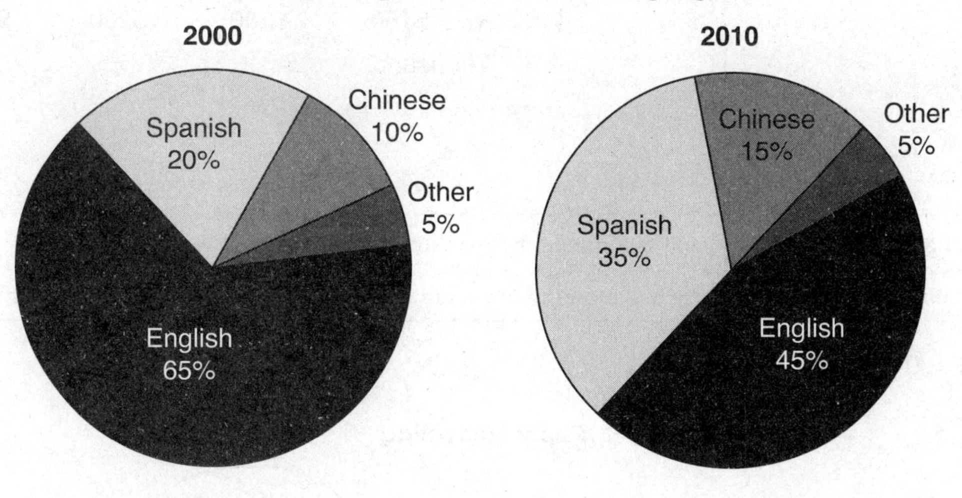

2

The graph below gives information about average housing prices throughout the city of Plimsburgh.

Summarize the information by selecting and reporting the main features, and make comparisons where relevant.

Write at least 150 words.

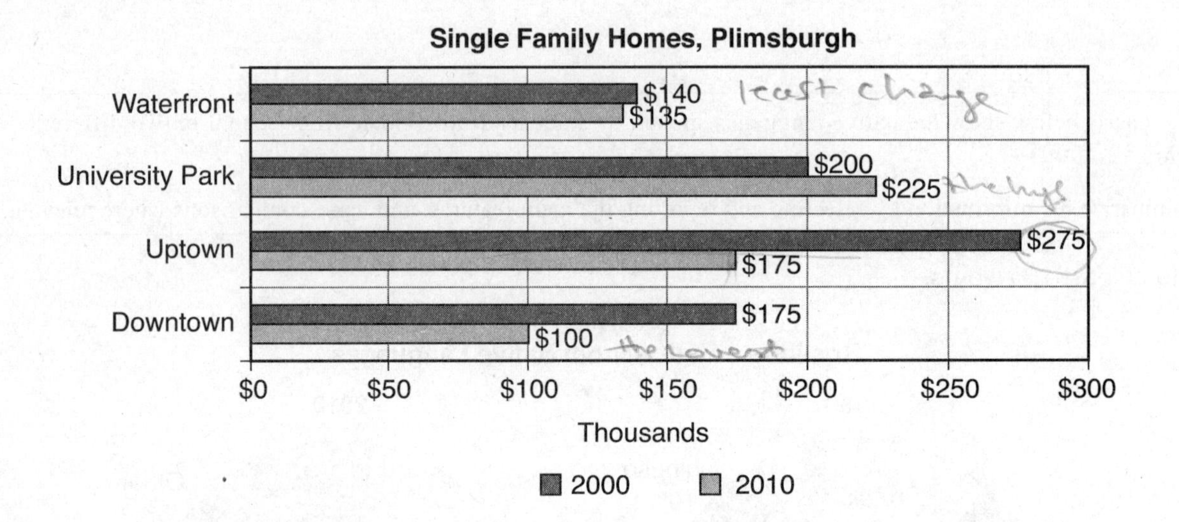

3

The diagram below shows the steps and equipment involved in recycling paper.

Summarize the information by selecting and reporting the main features, and make comparisons where relevant.

Write at least 150 words.

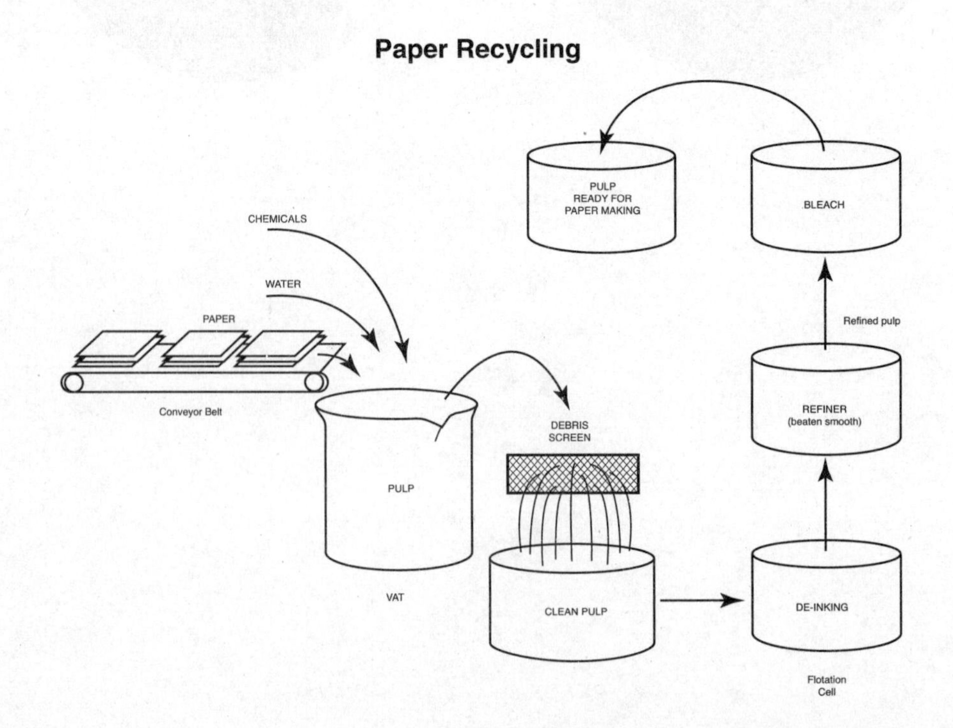

TASK 2

In Task 2, you will be asked for your opinion. Read the task carefully. You may be asked to describe the advantages and disadvantages of something or to discuss two different views of something. Make sure you address all parts of the task.

You will have forty minutes to write 250 words. Judge your time carefully.

There should be three parts to your response to the task. You will need enough time to plan and write each part. The most important part is the introduction. If you plan your introduction well, the rest of the essay will follow easily.

Introduction

Restate the Task

STRATEGY In the first sentence of the Introduction, you should restate the task.

You can restate Task 2 by paraphrasing it.

TIP Spend time planning your essay. Don't just start writing. Read the task carefully. Think about what the task asks you to do and how you will answer it.

PRACTICE 1 (answers on page 217)

Read the following tasks. Paraphrase the task using synonyms for the underlined word or phrases. The first exercise has been done for you.

1

In some school systems, children start learning at least one foreign language in primary school. In other school systems, foreign language education begins in secondary school.

In your opinion, should children learn foreign languages in schools, and if so, at what age should they begin?

Give reasons for your answer and include any relevant examples from your own knowledge or experience.

Paraphrase

It is important for children to study foreign languages in school.

2

Some people believe that it is cruel to test drugs and other new products on animals. Others believe that this sort of testing is important and necessary for improving and even saving people's lives.

Discuss both these views and give your own opinion.

Give reasons for your answer and include any relevant examples from your own knowledge or experience.

Paraphrase

....

3

Traditionally, elderly people have lived with and been cared for by younger family members. In modern society, more and more elderly people are living in special homes for the elderly. Why do you think families <u>choose</u> to have their <u>elderly relatives</u> live in special homes away from the family? What do you think is the best way for modern families to care for their elderly relatives?

Give reasons for your answer and include any relevant examples from your own knowledge or experience.

Paraphrase

....

4

Developing an area for tourism changes life in that area in many ways. What are some of the advantages and disadvantages that tourism can bring to the lives of <u>people who live in the area</u>?

Give reasons for your answer and include any relevant examples from your own knowledge or experience.

Paraphrase

....

5

Making smoking <u>illegal</u> is the best way to protect people from the <u>harmful effects</u> of tobacco. To what extent do you agree or disagree? What other measures do you think might be effective?

Give reasons for your answer and include any relevant examples from your own knowledge or experience.

Paraphrase

....

Give Your Opinion

STRATEGY In the second sentence of the Introduction, you should give your opinion.

TIP Your opinion does not have to be the second sentence, but until you get more confidence in writing, keep it the second sentence.

You can use these words and phrases when giving your opinion.

Useful Words and Phrases for Giving Opinions

I think	In my experience
I believe	In my opinion
I feel	It is my belief that
I consider	From my of point of view

PRACTICE 2 (answers on page 217)

Read the second sentence of the following Introductions. Add a word or phrase from the above list to express your opinion. The first exercise has been done for you.

1 It is important for children to study foreign languages in school. It is my belief that they should begin this at a very early age.

2 Some people feel that experimenting with drugs on animals is unkind, while others believe that it is crucial for making people's lives better. .... this sort of testing is cruel and unnecessary.

3 There are several reasons why families opt to have their older family members live in special homes. .... , however, elderly relatives should stay living with their family whenever possible.

4 Tourism brings both advantages and disadvantages to local residents. .... the benefits it can bring are greater than any drawbacks.

5 I agree that the best way to protect people from the dangers of smoking is to make it against the law. .... this is the only way to get people to stop smoking.

Write a Thesis Statement

STRATEGY	In the third sentence of the Introduction, you should write a thesis statement. This thesis statement tells the reader what ideas you will write to support your opinion.
TIP	You should have at least two main ideas. Three would be better, but two are enough.

PRACTICE 3 (answers on page 217)

Read the thesis statements. Which task in Practice 1 best matches the thesis statement? Write the task number in the blank. The first exercise has been done for you.

A ..2.. It may help scientists find ways to cure diseases, but it is painful for the animals and it is not the only way to test drugs.

B .... It would make it extremely difficult to obtain and use tobacco, and it would get people's attention.

C .... Children enjoy language, they learn it best when they are young, and language instruction fits in well with the rest of the primary school curriculum.

D .... It may be difficult for families to find time and energy to care for their elderly relatives, but it is the kinder thing to do and it is also more economical.

E .... Tourism can change the character of a place in undesirable ways, but it gives residents economic opportunities that they wouldn't have otherwise.

Body

Expand Your Thesis Statement

STRATEGY Use your thesis statement to write a topic sentence for each paragraph. The first sentence of each paragraph of the body of the essay is the topic sentence. The topic sentence shows how you will support your opinion.

TIP You should have at least two paragraphs in the body of your essay. Three would be better, but two are enough. Don't forget to indent.

PRACTICE 4 (answers on page 217)

Read each thesis statement and the sentences that follow it. Which are appropriate topic sentences for the body of the essay? Circle the correct letters. There may be more than one answer. The first exercise has been done for you.

1

Thesis Statement

If smoking were illegal, it would be extremely difficult to obtain and use tobacco, and it would get people's attention.

Topic Sentences

A A tax on cigarettes would make them too expensive for most people to buy.
(B) Even if people had cigarettes, it would be hard to find a place to smoke.
(C) People may choose to have bad habits, but most people won't choose to break the law.
D Smoking is prohibited in many public places these days.
(E) If smoking were illegal, then people wouldn't be able to buy cigarettes easily.

2

Thesis Statement

Children enjoy language, they learn it best when they are young, and language instruction fits in well with the rest of the primary school curriculum.

Topic Sentences

A Everyone knows that childhood is the best time to learn foreign languages.
B Young children enjoy learning and playing with language.
C Most children have a large vocabulary by the age of five.
D Some children are better than others at learning languages.
E Most of the things children learn in primary school are related to language.

3

Thesis Statement

It may be difficult for families to find time and energy to care for their elderly relatives, but it is the kinder thing to do, and it is also more economical.

Topic Sentences

A Elderly people often need more medical attention than younger people do.
B Homes for the elderly are very expensive.
C Elderly people have less energy than younger people do.
D People who have jobs and children don't have much time to care for elderly relatives.
E Our elderly relatives deserve to be treated kindly.

4

Thesis Statement

It may help scientists find ways to cure diseases, but it is painful for the animals and it is not the only way to test drugs.

Topic Sentences

A There are other equally effective ways to do experiments.
B Scientists seeking to cure diseases often use animals as part of their research.
C Some people will not buy products from companies that use animal testing.
D These sorts of experiments are often painful for the animals.
E Animal testing is done with beauty products as well as with drugs.

5

Thesis Statement

Tourism can change the character of a place in undesirable ways, but it gives residents economic opportunities that they wouldn't have otherwise.

Topic Sentences

A Tourism means traveling for recreational purposes.
B Tourism is a growing industry in many parts of the world.
C Tourism can change quiet towns into busy, crowded, expensive places.
D Tourism creates new possibilities for businesses and jobs.
E Tourism offices provide information for visitors new to an area.

Introduce Details

STRATEGY Use transition words and phrases to introduce and prioritize the details that support your topic sentence.

TIP Don't repeat the same transition words or phrases in your essay. Use a variety of transition words in each paragraph.

Common Transition Words and Phrases

first	second	so	additionally
in the first place	in the second place	therefore	furthermore
the main advantage is	then	however	moreover
another advantage	also	on the other hand	finally
another reason	and	but	
another	or	in addition	

PRACTICE 5 (answers on page 217)

Read each paragraph below. Underline the topic sentence. Complete each blank with a transition word or phrase from the above list. The first exercise has been done for you.

1 Everyone knows that childhood is the best time to learn foreign languages. **A** In the first place, it is the best time to learn anything because it is the time of life when the brain is developing. **B** ...., children are still developing skills in their native language when they are young, so their minds are open to learning language. **C** ...., children can learn to speak several languages fluently but it is more difficult for adults to do this.

2 People who have jobs and children don't have much time to care for elderly relatives. **A** ...., they spend most of the day at work. **B** ...., in their free time they have to take care of their children. **C** ...., they have to shop, clean, and do other housework. After taking care of these responsibilities, there is not a lot of time and energy left over.

3 There are other equally effective ways to do experiments. Drugs can be tested on humans, as they often already are. **A** ...., scientists use computer models as part of their research, and they often get more reliable results this way. **B** ...., scientists can use blood and cell samples from humans for their experiments. These methods are all more humane than using live animals.

4 Tourism can change quiet towns into busy, crowded, expensive places. **A** ...., hotels, restaurants, and roads have to be built to accommodate tourists. **B** ...., when the tourists arrive, they crowd the streets and public places. **C** ...., tourism usually means that prices in stores and restaurants go up. All these things change the quality of life for local residents.

5 Even if people had cigarettes, it would be hard to find a place to smoke. **A** ...., they wouldn't be able to smoke in any public place without getting arrested. **B** ...., they couldn't smoke in their own homes without leaving an odor. **C** ...., they wouldn't be able to smoke at their friends' houses without putting their friends in danger of arrest. A lot of people would quit smoking just because they couldn't find a place to do it.

STRATEGY REVIEW

Plan Your Essay

(answers on page 221)

Read the tasks below and make an outline to respond to the task. The first exercise is done for you.

1

In some places, workers are required to retire at a specific age. In other places, workers can retire when they choose.

In your opinion, should there be a mandatory retirement age for all workers?

Give reasons for your answer and include any relevant examples from your own knowledge or experience.

INTRODUCTION
TASK PARAPHRASE *People should not have to stop working at any specific age.*
MY OPINION *This is unfair and unnecessary.*
MY THESIS STATEMENT **Main Idea 1** *Some people enjoy working.*
Main Idea 2 *Some people need to keep earning money.*
Main Idea 3 *Everybody needs to feel a purpose in life.*

BODY 1
MAIN IDEA 1 *Some people enjoy working.*
Supporting Detail 1 *They may like the kind of work they do.*
Supporting Detail 2 *They may enjoy interacting with their colleagues.*
Supporting Detail 3 *They may like to feel they are part of something.*

BODY 2
MAIN IDEA 2 *Some people need to keep earning money.*
Supporting Detail 1 *They don't have savings or a pension.*
Supporting Detail 2 *Their savings or pension doesn't cover expenses.*
Supporting Detail 3 *They need money for medical expenses.*

BODY 3
MAIN IDEA 3 *Everybody needs to feel a purpose in life.*
Supporting Detail 1 *A job gives a person a sense of purpose.*
Supporting Detail 2 *A job makes a person feel useful.*
Supporting Detail 3 *A job makes a person feel like she is contributing.*

CONCLUSION
TASK PARAPHRASE *Some people want to stop working at a certain time while others want to work longer.*
MY OPINION *It is not right to make everyone retire at the same age.*

2

> Many students choose to complete at least some part of their university studies in a foreign country.
>
> What are some of the advantages and disadvantages of studying abroad?

Give reasons for your answer and include any relevant examples from your own knowledge or experience.

INTRODUCTION
TASK PARAPHRASE ....
MY OPINION ....
MY THESIS STATEMENT **Main Idea 1** ....
Main Idea 2 ....
Main Idea 3 ....

BODY 1
MAIN IDEA 1 ....
Supporting Detail 1 ....
Supporting Detail 2 ....
Supporting Detail 3 ....

BODY 2
MAIN IDEA 2 ....
Supporting Detail 1 ....
Supporting Detail 2 ....
Supporting Detail 3 ....

BODY 3
MAIN IDEA 3 ....
Supporting Detail 1 ....
Supporting Detail 2 ....
Supporting Detail 3 ....

CONCLUSION
TASK PARAPHRASE ....
MY OPINION ....

3

> Some schools require their students to wear uniforms because they believe it helps the students focus on their schoolwork rather than on their clothes.
>
> Discuss this view and give your own opinion.

Give reasons for your answer and include any relevant examples from your own knowledge or experience.

INTRODUCTION
TASK PARAPHRASE ....
MY OPINION ....
MY THESIS STATEMENT **Main Idea 1** ....
Main Idea 2 ....
Main Idea 3 ....

BODY 1
MAIN IDEA 1 ....
Supporting Detail 1 ....
Supporting Detail 2 ....
Supporting Detail 3 ....

BODY 2
MAIN IDEA 2 ....
Supporting Detail 1 ....
Supporting Detail 2 ....
Supporting Detail 3 ....

BODY 3
MAIN IDEA 3 ....
Supporting Detail 1 ....
Supporting Detail 2 ....
Supporting Detail 3 ....

CONCLUSION
TASK PARAPHRASE ....
MY OPINION ....

4

Zoos should be banned because it is cruel to keep wild animals in captivity. To what extent do you agree or disagree with this statement?

Give reasons for your answer and include any relevant examples from your own knowledge or experience.

INTRODUCTION

TASK PARAPHRASE ....

MY OPINION ....

MY THESIS STATEMENT **Main Idea 1** ....

Main Idea 2 ....

Main Idea 3 ....

BODY 1

MAIN IDEA 1 ....

Supporting Detail 1 ....

Supporting Detail 2 ....

Supporting Detail 3 ....

BODY 2

MAIN IDEA 2 ....

Supporting Detail 1 ....

Supporting Detail 2 ....

Supporting Detail 3 ....

BODY 3

MAIN IDEA 3 ....

Supporting Detail 1 ....

Supporting Detail 2 ....

Supporting Detail 3 ....

CONCLUSION

TASK PARAPHRASE ....

MY OPINION ....

5

> These days, more and more people eat prepared meals from restaurants and grocery stores instead of cooking for themselves.
>
> What do you think are the reasons for this trend?
>
> To what extent do you think this is a positive trend?

Give reasons for your answer and include any relevant examples from your own knowledge or experience.

INTRODUCTION
TASK PARAPHRASE ....
MY OPINION ....
MY THESIS STATEMENT **Main Idea 1** ....
Main Idea 2 ....
Main Idea 3 ....

BODY 1
MAIN IDEA 1 ....
Supporting Detail 1 ....
Supporting Detail 2 ....
Supporting Detail 3 ....

BODY 2
MAIN IDEA 2 ....
Supporting Detail 1 ....
Supporting Detail 2 ....
Supporting Detail 3 ....

BODY 3
MAIN IDEA 3 ....
Supporting Detail 1 ....
Supporting Detail 2 ....
Supporting Detail 3 ....

CONCLUSION
TASK PARAPHRASE ....
MY OPINION ....

Write Your Essay

(answers on page 224)

Take the outlines you wrote for the five topics above and create an essay for each one. Model essays are in the answer key, but remember your answers will vary. Use your own paper.

....

....

....

....

....

....

....

....

....

....

....

....

....

....

....

....

....

....

....

Revise Your Essay

After you write, take a few minutes to reread your essay to check the organization and correct grammar and spelling if necessary.

Do not make major changes. You don't have time. Make small corrections as necessary.

IELTS SPEAKING MODULE

OVERVIEW

In this chapter, you will learn and practice specific strategies based on the different tasks in the three parts of the Speaking Module. You also will review the importance of key words that you learned in the first chapter of this book. You will learn how these key words will help you answer the questions in the Speaking Module.

At the end of this chapter, you will find a Strategy Review that is similar to the actual IELTS Speaking test.

Speaking Tips

There are some general tips that will help you during the Speaking Module.

1. Keep talking. The examiner needs to hear you use English. Don't be shy.
2. Don't worry about small mistakes. You will make mistakes, but don't worry about them. Even native speakers make mistakes. Correct your mistakes if you can and keep talking.
3. Don't try to memorize responses. Just speak spontaneously and naturally.
4. Don't worry about a particular Part. Your score is a composite of all three Parts, not just one.
5. Take advantage of your preparation time in Part 2.
6. Don't worry if the examiner stops you. Each part has a time limit.

Part	Total Time	Preparation Time
	11–14 minutes	
1	4–5 minutes	none
2	3–4 minutes	1 minute
3	4–5 minutes	none

Part 1—General Questions About Yourself and Everyday Situations

The examiner will ask you a few questions on two or three topics. You may be asked to talk about your family, food, school, work, neighborhood, your home town, or other similar topics.

Everday Vocabulary

STRATEGY 1	Know the vocabulary to talk about yourself and everyday situations.
TIP	Don't give short answers. Give one or two sentence answers. Don't memorize answers. Knowing nouns and adjectives for each of the topics will be very helpful.

PRACTICE 1 (answers on page 227)

Listen to these IELTS test takers answer the examiner's questions. Write the missing words in the blanks. Then write your own answer to the examiner's question.

Family

Question 1: Tell me something about your family.

1 I have a .... family. There is my mother and father. Plus I have two .... brothers and a .... sister.

2 I have a .... family, just me and my mother and father. But my .... and aunts and .... live very nearby, so we seem like a .... family.

3 I recently got married, and my .... and I live alone in a small apartment. But her .... live nearby, and she has lots of .... She is very .... to her family.

4 I have a .... brother. He is my only sibling, so ours is a .... family. Most of our relatives live in another city, so we don't see them often. We have some .... cousins who live near us, but I don't know them well.

5 **YOU:** ....
....
....

Question 2: What do you enjoy doing with your family?

1 My brothers and sisters and I all enjoy ...., so we spend a lot of time playing soccer and tennis together. Also, we usually .... our cousins every weekend and have a big .... with them.

2 We all like to .... in our family, and we really enjoy .... books together. We don't always have the same .... about books, so we argue a lot. It may sound ...., but we think that's really fun.

3 We usually take a big family .... every summer. We .... a big house at the beach and .... all our cousins to stay with us.

4 Unfortunately, I am usually too .... to spend much time with my family because of my job. But I visit my parents when I can. My mother .... a nice dinner for me, and we sit around and .... about things. It's quiet and ....

5 **YOU:** ....
....
....

Question 3: Do you prefer spending time with your family or with friends?

1 I like spending time with both family and friends. But to tell the truth, I have more .... with my friends. My friends and I .... a lot of .... That's why they're my friends.

2 I have a new ...., so I don't have much time for friends. He takes most of my .... For now, my friends are my .... and my son. That's .... with me.

3 I really enjoy spending time with my family. My brothers and sisters and I enjoy many of the same .... We have a lot ....

4 I have a lot of friends, and I enjoy spending time with them. We go out together in large .... My friends are .... a large family to me. I .... better with my friends than I do with my family.

5 **YOU:** ....
....
....

Food

Question 1: What kinds of food do you prefer to eat?

1 I like .... all kinds of food. I especially like .... from .... countries. I always enjoy trying food that is new and ....

2 I like the .... my mother cooks. She cooks food that is .... in our country. It's really .... Nobody cooks as .... as my mother does.

3 I am a ...., so I never eat meat. I prefer food that's .... with .... vegetables. I eat a lot of ...., too.

4 I generally prefer to eat beef or .... with .... And I love .... I like anything that's .... I almost never eat ....

5 **YOU:** ....

Question 2: Do you usually eat at home or at restaurants?

1 I almost always eat at restaurants because I am .... all day. I always have .... at a .... When I have to work late, which is often, I usually buy a .... to eat in the office. That's my dinner.

2 I always eat .... and .... at home, and I eat lunch at home, too, when I can. But on ...., I often go to restaurants with my friends.

3 I usually eat at home because it's too .... to eat at restaurants. I only .... a meal at a restaurant when it's a .... , for example, someone's birthday.

4 I eat at home because it's more .... I have three children, so it's easier for us to eat at home. Also, there aren't many good restaurants in my .... I think the food we eat at home .... better.

5 **YOU:** ....

Question 3: What is your favorite restaurant?

1 My favorite restaurant is a small place near my house. It .... the most delicious .... It's a great place to go for an afternoon .... I .... meet my friends there.

2 There is a very .... restaurant downtown that has French food. I had my .... dinner there last year. The .... are high, so I can't go there very often, but I really like it.

3 I like to go to a .... restaurant near my school. I don't usually have a lot of time for lunch so it's a good place for me. I can get a .... or a sandwich there and eat it .... It's ...., too.

4 My favorite restaurant is a .... restaurant near my house. I like it because I like .... It has lots of other kinds of food on the ...., too.

5 **YOU:** ....

Hometown

Question 1: Tell me something about your hometown.

1 My hometown is very .... and .... We only have a few stores and one movie theater. It's a .... place to live, but it isn't very .... The .... is small, so everyone knows everyone else.

2 I come from a .... city. It's a very .... place. The streets are always .... A lot of .... people live and work there.

3 My hometown is in the .... There is a lot of beautiful .... around it, so tourists like to visit. It's a ....-sized city, but during the summer it .... up with visitors.

4 I come from a .... outside a large city. It's a .... place, but there isn't much to do there. Everybody goes to the city to .... or look for ....

5 **YOU:** ....
....
....

Question 2: What do you like about your hometown?

1 People come from all over the .... to work and .... in my city. You can always .... interesting people there. I really like that.

2 My town is a very .... place. There are lots of gardens and .... In the spring, it's very .... when all the flowers bloom. In fact, my town is .... for its flowers.

3 There are a lot of .... for both work and study in my hometown. We have several .... Also, since it's a big city, there are a lot of ...., and it's .... to find a job.

4 My town is a very quiet and .... place. That's why it's a good place to .... a family. There is very little .... in my town.

5 **YOU:** ....
....
....

Question 3: What is something you don't like about your hometown?

1 My town can be a very .... place to be. There aren't many things to do there. Everything is always the .... Nothing ever ....

2 I come from a big city, and there is a lot of .... on the streets. Because of that, the streets are always ...., and the air is .... I don't really like that, but I guess it's the same in every big city in the world.

3 My hometown is in a very cold .... We have long, dark .... It can get very .... I think I would .... to live in a .... place.

4 Everything in my hometown is very .... It costs a lot to rent an .... It costs a lot to buy food or to ride the .... If you don't have a good job, you can't .... to live there.

5 **YOU:** ....

....

....

School

Question 1: What was your high school like?

1 I went to a very small high school. When I ...., there were only forty students in my class. Because the school was so small, we didn't study a large .... of subjects. However, I had some very .... teachers, and I learned a lot from them.

2 My high school was .... The classrooms were always .... We had a good .... program, and I played on several ....

3 I went to an .... high school. I'm sure it was like most other high schools. We studied the .... subjects and did the same kinds of .... that high school students do everywhere. I was on the .... team, and I was a member of the computer ....

4 My high school was in a .... building. Everything in the school was new. We had a beautiful .... and a large .... We had all new .... for our science classes. It was a great place to go to school.

5 **YOU:** ....

....

....

Question 2: What was your favorite subject in high school?

1 I really enjoyed my .... class. I've always liked ...., and I think biology is .... interesting. I liked learning about .... and ....

2 I always liked .... classes best. I took an art class every year I was in high school. Maybe I'm not a very .... artist, but I enjoy painting and .... and things like that.

3 .... was .... my favorite subject in high school. I wasn't the .... student in this subject. In fact, it has always been .... for me, but I like it anyhow.

4 I liked studying .... a lot. I think it's the most .... subject. I still read about it often. I like .... about how things were in the ....

5 **YOU:** ....

Question 3: What advice do you have for high school students today?

1 They should .... hard, of course, and .... to their teachers. What students learn in high school is very important for the ...., so they should take it ....

2 I think high school students should remember to enjoy their .... When they ...., they will have a lot of .... , so they should .... during their high school years.

3 High school students .... to start thinking about their future .... They should study subjects that will help them later on at the .... and in their jobs. High school is a time to .... for the future.

4 I think high school students should study a lot of different .... They need to .... what things interest them. The only way to know is to .... different things.

5 **YOU:** ....

Transportation

Question 1: What is transportation like in your city or town?

1 I live in a big city, so we have a lot of .... and .... People also .... their cars, but the traffic .... slowly because the streets are so crowded.

2 I live in a small town, and we don't have any .... transportation. People usually drive their own .... We have a ...., but that's for .... travel.

3 In my city, people usually .... the bus or use their cars. Also, a lot of people ride .... We have special bicycle .... on some of the bigger streets.

4 We have a lot of transportation .... in my city. We have subways and buses and .... If you live and work downtown, you can .... everywhere you need to go. Our downtown .... are always busy.

5 **YOU:** ....
....
....

Question 2: How do you usually get to school or work?

1 I usually drive to school because my school is .... from my house. It .... me about an hour to get there. I usually .... to some of my classmates, so the trip isn't boring.

2 I take the subway to work. The .... is about a ten-............................ walk from my apartment. It's very ....

3 I always walk to school. It takes .... an hour. It's a good way to get ...., but I have to leave my house early in order to get to school ....

4 I ride the bus to work. The .... is very close to my house. I have to .... to another bus downtown.

5 **YOU:** ....
....
....

Question 3: Are there any problems with your transportation to school or work?

1 My biggest problem is that I have to .... a lot of money to put .... in my car. Also, it takes a long time to get to school from my house. But the only .... to those problems would be to find an apartment .... to my school.

2 I don't really have any problems with taking the subway. It's very .... The only thing is that the subway .... is high, and it costs more during ....

3 I don't have any problems with .... to school. I really enjoy it. It takes a long time, but I don't .... For me, it's ....

4 The biggest problems with transportation in my city is the .... It takes a long time to .... anywhere because of that. It doesn't matter if you .... the bus or .... a car. Traffic is always a problem.

5 **YOU:** ....
....
....

Weather

Question 1: What is the weather like in your city or town?

1 In my town we have four ...., so the weather .... on the time of year. It .... a lot, from very .... to very ...., and everything in between.

2 I live in a .... part of the world, so the weather is always .... in my city. We have two seasons—............................ and .... During the rainy season, it rains in the afternoons, but the mornings are usually ....

3 My city is in the far north, so we have .... weather. The .... aren't cold, but they are very short. The .... are long, and we get a lot of ....

4 We have a very .... climate in my town. The weather is usually .... The .... never gets too high or too low.

5 **YOU:** ....
....
....

Question 2: What do you like to do when the weather is rainy?

1 I love rainy weather. I like to make a hot cup of .... and get a good book and sit by the .... listening to the .... on the glass.

2 I feel .... when the weather is rainy. Everything seems gray and .... and .... I don't like to do anything when it rains. I just .... that the weather will .... soon.

3 This may sound funny, but I like to go .... when it rains. I like to feel the rain .... on me, and I like to walk through the .... But, if it's raining ...., I stay ....

4 I don't do anything .... in rainy weather. I don't .... about it, except if there's a big .... If there's .... and lightning, I feel .... I don't like that at all.

5 **YOU:** ....
....
....

Question 3: What kind of climate would you prefer to live in?

1 I would love to live where the .... is always .... because I don't like to feel .... I like to go outside every day and enjoy the ....

2 I would like to live in a place that has a .... winter with .... of snow. That's because I love to .... I enjoy all winter ...., so I'd like to live where I could do them easily.

3 I like living in a place that has four seasons. Each one .... something different. .... and .... are very pretty times of year. Summer always has .... weather. I even like the .... and snow in the winter.

4 I don't like .... days, so I would like to live in a dry climate, maybe even near a .... I'd like to live in a place where the sun always .... and there are never any .... in the sky.

5 **YOU:** ....

Exercise

Question 1: What kinds of physical exercise do you like to do?

1 I play soccer, so that's the main way I .... exercise. I also try to .... at least a few times a week to .... for soccer.

2 I like to ride my ...., but I don't do it very often. I also play .... sometimes when I can find someone to play with. I guess I'm not a very .... person.

3 I like to .... at the gym. That's my .... way to exercise. Sometimes I ...., also, but the .... at the gym is often crowded and I don't like that.

4 I enjoy .... I take classes, and I also .... at home. It's a good way to .... up your ....

5 **YOU:** ....

Question 2: What kind of exercise did you do when you were younger?

1 When I was in school, I .... on several different sports .... I really enjoyed .... sports then. I .... a lot more exercise then than I do now.

2 I .... walk to school every day when I was younger. In addition, I .... tennis ...., and I also played volleyball. I had a lot of .... then.

3 I played .... a lot when I was younger. I wasn't very .... it, but I really liked it. I always .... a good time, even if my team lost.

4 When I was a child, I spent a lot of time outside with my friends. We didn't do any .... kinds of exercise. We just played a lot of different games. We .... and .... a lot as part of our games.

5 **YOU:** ....

Question 3: Is exercise important to you? Why or why not?

1 I think it's important to exercise .... Unfortunately, I don't exercise often .... I always feel better after exercise, but I get .... about it sometimes.

2 I try to exercise every day. It's really important for my .... I try to eat a good ...., too. I think that's the reason why I am almost never ....

3 I think exercise is good, but I am usually .... for it. I don't have a lot of ...., and when I do have time, I prefer to ....

4 I don't like exercise at all. I just think it's really .... I can think of lots of better ways to .... time. I would .... go to the movies or be with my friends, for example.

5 **YOU:** ....

Verb Tense

Many of the questions in Part 1 are about the present, but the examiner may also ask you about the past and the future. Be sure to give the information that the examiner asks for.

STRATEGY	Pay close attention to the verb tense that the examiner uses.
TIP	Listen for tense markers in the examiner's question.

Common Tense Markers

Present	now, at this moment, presently, do/does, these days, usually
Past	in the past, when you were younger, when you were a child, before, did
Future	in the future, in a few years, later, will

PRACTICE 2 (answers on page 228)

Listen to these IELTS examiner's questions. Underline the tense markers in the examiner's question. Then choose the answer that matches the tense of the question.

Family

Question 1: When you were younger, did you spend more time with family or with friends?

A I spent most of my free time with my friends.
B I spend more time with my family these days.

Question 2: In the past, did you spend more or less time with your family than you do now?

A I spend almost every weekend with my parents.
B I spent a lot more time with my family.

Question 3: Do you ask your family for help when you have a problem?

A Yes, I always talked to my family when I had a problem.
B Yes, my parents are always the first people I talk to when I have a problem.

Food

Question 1: What did you like to eat when you were younger?

A I will probably eat more vegetables and fewer sweets.
B I loved to eat sweet things like ice cream and cookies.

Question 2: Who usually does the cooking in your house?

A My mother cooks most of our meals.
B My mother cooked for us every day.

Question 3: Did you eat at restaurants often when you were a child?

A No, we almost always ate at home.
B No, I rarely eat at restaurants.

Hometown

Question 1: Do you think you will live in your hometown later on?

A I lived in my hometown with my family until I got married.
B I won't live in my hometown after I finish school because there are few job opportunities there.

Question 2: What did you like about your hometown when you were a child?

A I like the variety of stores and restaurants that we have.
B I liked playing in the park with my friends.

Question 3: How do you think life in your hometown will be different in the future?

A I think my hometown will be busier and more crowded because the population is growing rapidly.
B I think my hometown is a very pleasant place to live.

Work

Question 1: Why did you choose your profession?

A I chose to be a doctor because my father was also a doctor.
B I enjoy my work as a doctor very much.

Question 2: What do you like most about the job you have now?

A I will help people who need it.
B I like having the chance to help other people.

Question 3: Do you think you will have a different kind of job in the future?

A I think I will always be a doctor.
B I worked as an office assistant right after I finished high school.

Transportation

Question 1: How did you get to school when you were a child?

A I prefer to walk to school.
B I always took the bus to school.

Question 2: Will you buy a car when you start working?

A No, I will probably continue traveling by bus and subway.
B No, I didn't, because it was too expensive.

Question 3: Do many people in your city ride the buses?

A Yes, they rode the buses a lot.
B Yes, most people ride the buses to work.

Weather

Question 1: What kind of weather do you dislike?

A I really dislike very hot days because they make me feel so tired.
B I used to dislike snowy weather, but now I like it.

Question 2: How does the weather affect your mood?

A I always feel very happy when the sun is shining.
B I will be very happy if it snows soon.

Question 3: What was your favorite season when you were a child?

A Summer is my favorite season because I like to be outdoors.
B I always loved the winter because I enjoyed playing in the snow.

Exercise

Question 1: Do you think your exercise habits will change in the future?

A I have very good exercise habits.
B I will probably have less time to exercise when I start working.

Question 2: How often do you exercise?

A I swim or play tennis at least twice a week.
B I will probably ride my bike every weekend.

Question 3: Did you exercise differently in the past?

A I usually take a walk in the morning.
B I used to run everyday, but I don't anymore.

3. to
4. from
5. to
6. from
7. to
8. by

Comparisons

PRACTICE 3

1. busier
2. higher
3. lower
4. more
5. more
6. fewer
7. more; higher
8. higher

Plurals

PRACTICE 4

1. salaries
2. doctors
3. years
4. salary
5. woman
6. doctor
7. man
8. years
9. rate
10. salaries
11. women
12. men
13. rate
14. men
15. women

Articles

PRACTICE 5

1. 0
2. 0
3. a
4. a
5. the
6. 0
7. 0
8. 0
9. the
10. a
11. The
12. the

Subject–Verb Agreement

PRACTICE 6

1. shows
2. spend
3. spend
4. take
5. spends
6. is
7. takes
8. take
9. account
10. shows
11. spend
12. is

Verb Tenses

PRACTICE 7

1. spent
2. went
3. took
4. went
5. has increased
6. has remained
7. has decreased
8. will spend
9. will rise
10. will stay
11. will drop
12. spends

Spelling

The graph gives information about ~~litracy~~ literacy rates in two ~~countrys~~ countries over a period of ~~sevral~~ several centuries, from 1700 until 2000. While the literacy rates in both ~~countrys~~ countries ~~incresed~~ increased in each century, the rates in Country X remained higher than in Country Y in every year shown.

In 1700, more than 40 percent of the ~~popalation~~ population in Country X was literate. In Country Y, however, a much smaller ~~percenage~~ percentage of the people could read. In fact, the ~~litracy~~ literacy rate was ~~amost~~ almost zero. ~~Allthough~~ Although the number of people who could read grew in both ~~contrys~~ countries over the next centuries, the ~~litrcy~~ literacy rate in Country Y remained low. By 1900 only about 30 percent of the people in that country could read, while the ~~litrcy~~ literacy rate in Country X in the same year was well over 80 percent.

By 2000, the last year shown on the graph, 100 percent of the people in Country X could read. The ~~litrcy~~ literacy rate in Country Y had ~~reeched~~ reached 80 percent, but this was still low as ~~compard~~ compared with Country X.

CHECK AND REVISE

2. The opening statement is complete. It paraphrases the task and makes it more specific with information about both time and location. Important data are included and one trend is described—the difference between sales in 2011 and 2012. The other trend—the months when sales were highest and lowest—is not described but only given a brief mention in the concluding paragraph. More details and analysis of this trend should be included earlier in the response. The final sentence is an opinion, not a fact, so shouldn't be included. At 150 words, this response is a good length.
3. The opening statement is incomplete. It is missing information about location (Wardsville). The important trends—the different proportions of time teachers spend in different activities—are described and compared. The second sentence of the last paragraph is an opinion, not a fact, so shouldn't be included. At 158 words, this response is a good length.
4. The opening statement is complete. It paraphrases the task and mentions both the diagrams. All the important steps of the process diagram and all the important features of the structure diagram are mentioned. Two important pieces of information are missing—the temperature of the ocean required for a hurricane to form, and the minimum wind speed of a hurricane. At 121 words, this response is too short.

STRATEGY REVIEW

Model answers

1. The charts show the percentage of Roslindale High school students who spoke different native languages in 2000 and 2010.

   In 2000, the largest group of students—sixty-five percent—spoke English as their native language. Spanish speakers made up the next largest group. Twenty percent of students spoke that language. Ten percent spoke Chinese and five percent spoke other languages.

   The sizes of the different language groups changed in 2010. Native English speakers still made up the largest group, but the percentage of these students shrank from sixty-five percent to forty-five percent. In the meantime, the number of Spanish speakers grew to thirty-five percent and the number of Chinese speakers grew to fifteen percent. Speakers of other languages made up five percent of the population, the same as in 2000.

   Overall, the charts show that at Roslindale High School, the percentage of students who speak English is decreasing while the percentage who speak Spanish and Chinese is increasing.

2. The graph shows the average prices of single family homes in four different neighborhoods in the city of Plimsburgh during 2000 and 2010. In all but one neighborhood, prices were lower in 2010 than they had been in 2000.

   In 2000, the most expensive place to live in Plimsburgh was the Uptown neighborhood, where the average price of a single family home was $275,000. The least expensive neighborhood was Waterfront. The average price of a single family home there was $140,000.

   By 2010, prices had fallen in all neighborhoods except University Park. There, the price of a single family home had increased from $200,000 to $225,000, and this neighborhood became the most expensive one in Plimsburgh. The downtown neighborhood became the least expensive one in 2010. Prices there plummeted to $100,000 for a single family home in that year. The neighborhood with the least change in price was Waterfront. The average housing price dropped by only $5,000 between 2000 and 2010.

3. The diagram shows the process of recycling paper and the equipment used to do this. Recycling paper involves the use of several vats as well as different kinds of chemicals, including bleach. The process begins when bales of paper are carried by a conveyer belt to a vat. In the vat, the paper is mixed together with water and chemicals to form pulp. After this, the pulp is pushed through a screen in order to remove any debris. Now the pulp is clean. It then moves into a flotation cell where it gets de-inked. Next, the de-inked pulp moves into a refiner. Here, it is beaten until it is smooth and refined. The refined pulp is transferred to a vat filled with bleach. Finally, after the pulp has been bleached, it is transferred to a new vat. Now the clean and bleached pulp is ready for use.

TASK 2

Introduction

Restate the Task

PRACTICE 1

Possible answers

2. Some people feel that experimenting with drugs on animals is unkind, while others believe that it is crucial for making people's lives better.
3. There are several reasons why families opt to have their older family members live in special homes.
4. Tourism brings both advantages and disadvantages to local residents.
5. I agree that the best way to protect people from the dangers of smoking is to make it against the law.

Give Your Opinion

PRACTICE 2

Possible answers

2. I believe this sort of testing is cruel and unnecessary.
3. I think, however, elderly relatives should stay living with their family whenever possible.
4. From my point of view, the benefits it can bring are greater than any drawbacks.
5. In my opinion, this is the only way to get people to stop smoking.

Write a Thesis Statement

PRACTICE 3

B. 5
C. 1
D. 3
E. 4

Body

Expand Your Thesis Statement

PRACTICE 4

2. A, B, E
3. B, D, E
4. A, B, D
5. C, D

Introduce Details

PRACTICE 5

Possible answers

1. B. In the second place
   C. Finally
2. **Topic sentence:** People who have jobs and children don't have much time to care for elderly relatives.
   A. First
   B. Then
   C. Additionally
3. **Topic sentence:** There are other equally effective ways to do experiments.
   A. In addition
   B. Moreover
4. **Topic sentence:** Tourism can change quiet towns into busy, crowded, expensive places.
   A. In the first place
   B. Then
   C. In addition
5. **Topic sentence:** Even if people had cigarettes, it would be hard to find a place to smoke.
   A. First
   B. Also
   C. Furthermore

Conclusion

Summarize Your Opinion

Practice 6

2. C
3. B
4. B
5. A

GRAMMAR

Gerunds and Infinitives

Practice 1

1. smoking
2. to smoke
3. to buy
4. to smoke
5. smoking
6. protecting
7. smoking

Modals

Practice 2

1. can't
2. may/might/could
3. can't
4. must
5. may/might/could
6. may/might/could
7. should

Active and Passive Voice

Practice 3

1. are looked
2. are kept
3. are fed
4. are treated
5. were treated
6. weren't given
7. were neglected
8. will be given

Relative Pronouns—Subject

Practice 4

1. who
2. which
3. that
4. which
5. that
6. whose
7. who

Relative Pronouns—Object

Practice 5

1. that
2. that
3. that
4. whom
5. which

Real Future Conditionals

Practice 6

1. study
2. will learn
3. wait
4. will be
5. will have
6. want

Unreal Conditionals

Practice 7

1. had had
2. would have studied
3. had studied
4. would have learned
5. knew
6. would read
7. spoke
8. would travel

PUNCTUATION

Apostrophes

Practice

Tourism brings many opportunities to the local residents. ~~Lets~~ Let's say, for example, that ~~your~~ you're a young person living in a small town near the beach. There aren't many jobs in the town. ~~You're~~ Your opportunities are very few. You probably think about moving to the city, where you have more ~~chance's~~ chances of getting a good job. Now ~~lets~~ let's say that your town decides to develop the area for tourism. Hotels, restaurants, and stores are built. The roads are improved. Now you and all ~~you're~~ your relatives and friends have many job opportunities in your own town. You can stay ~~they're~~ there and earn a good living. You can raise your family ~~they're~~ there knowing that your ~~childrens~~ children's opportunities for a good future are better now. I understand why some people think that tourism causes many problems, but I think ~~its~~ it's a good thing. It makes life better for local residents.

CHECK AND REVISE

PRACTICE 1

2

Introduction	Is the task paraphrased? yes/(no) **Comments:** The introduction begins with the writer's opinion. Also, the task asks the writer to discuss both views, but only one point of view is mentioned. Is an opinion given? (yes) / no **Comments:** .... Is there a thesis statement with two or three main ideas? (yes) / no **Comments:** ....
Body	Is there a paragraph for each of the main ideas? (yes) / no **Comments:** .... Does each paragraph have a topic sentence? (yes) / no **Comments:** .... Does each paragraph have two or three supporting details? yes/(no) **Comments:** The fourth paragraph doesn't have any supporting ideas.
Conclusion	Is the task paraphrased? yes/(no) **Comments:** Add a paraphrase of the task similar to: Whether drugs should be tested on animals or not is a major issue. Is the opinion restated? (yes) / no **Comments:** ....
Length	Is the response at least 250 words? yes/(no)

3

Introduction	Is the task paraphrased? (yes) / no **Comments:** .... Is an opinion given? (yes) / no **Comments:** .... Is there a thesis statement with two or three main ideas? yes/(no) **Comments:** Since there is no thesis statement, the main ideas aren't presented in the introduction, but there are three paragraphs and each has a main idea. The thesis statement should be something like this: Children are still learning their own language and are too young to recognize the need for being bilingual.
Body	Is there a paragraph for each of the main ideas? (yes) / no **Comments:** .... Does each paragraph have a topic sentence? (yes) / no **Comments:** .... Does each paragraph have two or three supporting details? (yes) / no **Comments:** ....

Conclusion	Is the task paraphrased? (yes) / no **Comments:** .... Is the opinion restated? yes/(no) **Comments:** Although I think that secondary language instruction should begin in secondary school, local schools can make the decision themselves.
Length	Is the response at least 250 words? (yes) / no

4

Introduction	Is the task paraphrased? yes/(no) **Comments:** The task is copied almost exactly. Is an opinion given? yes/(no) **Comments:** No opinion is stated. Suggestion: I believe the advantages outweigh the disadvantages. Is there a thesis statement with two or three main ideas? yes/(no) **Comments:** You could add more information to your opinion. I believe the advantages such as increased revenue and improved infrastructure outweigh the disadvantages.
Body	Is there a paragraph for each of the main ideas? (yes) / no **Comments:** .... Does each paragraph have a topic sentence? yes/(no) **Comments:** The paragraph about disadvantages does not have a topic sentence. Does each paragraph have two or three supporting details? (yes) / no **Comments:** ....
Conclusion	Is the task paraphrased? yes/(no) **Comments:** .... Is the opinion restated? yes/(no) **Comments:** It is stated for the first time.
Length	Is the response at least 250 words? yes/(no)

5

Introduction	Is the task paraphrased? (yes) / no **Comments:** .... Is an opinion given? (yes) / no **Comments:** .... Is there a thesis statement with two or three main ideas? yes/(no) **Comments:** The thesis statement only presents one main idea.

Body	Is there a paragraph for each of the main ideas? (yes) / no **Comments:** .... Does each paragraph have a topic sentence? (yes) / no **Comments:** .... Does each paragraph have two or three supporting details? (yes) / no **Comments:** ....
Conclusion	Is the task paraphrased? yes/ (no) **Comments:** There is no conclusion. Is the opinion restated? yes/ (no) **Comments:** A possible conclusion: Even though there are laws to regulate behavior, I believe that people will not change unless they change their habits, become educated about the problems, and get support from those around them.
Length	Is the response at least 250 words? (yes) / no

PRACTICE 2

2. Change *chilren* to *children*.
3. Change *activitys* to *activities*.
4. Change *want relax* to *want to relax*.
5. Change *food who you cook* to *food that you cook*.
6. Change *Its an important time* to *It's an important time*.
7. Change *chilren* to *children*.
8. Omit the comma after *children*.
9. Change *Their healthier* to *They're healthier*.
10. Change *Eat* to *Eating*.
11. Add a comma after *If more families cooked at home*.
12. Change *would have saved* to *would save*.

STRATEGY REVIEW

Plan Your Essay

Model answers

2

INTRODUCTION

TASK PARAPHRASE There are both benefits and drawbacks to studying abroad.

MY OPINION I feel that going to a university in a foreign country can be a valuable experience.

MY THESIS STATEMENT
Main Idea 1 Starting a career at home may be difficult.
Main Idea 2 It allows students to learn about another language and culture.
Main Idea 3 It provides educational opportunities.

BODY 1

MAIN IDEA 1 Starting a career at home may be difficult.

Supporting Detail 1 The student may not have had the right training.

Supporting Detail 2 She hasn't made professional connections.

Supporting Detail 3 These problems are easy to overcome.

BODY 2

MAIN IDEA 2 It allows students to learn about another language and culture.

Supporting Detail 1 Foreign language skills are important.

Supporting Detail 2 Understanding cultures is important.

Supporting Detail 3 These are advantages when looking for a job.

BODY 3

MAIN IDEA 3 It provides educational opportunities.

Supporting Detail 1 Their own country doesn't have good universities.

Supporting Detail 2 Another country has the best training for a certain profession.

Supporting Detail 3 The training they want is not available at home.

CONCLUSION

TASK PARAPHRASE There are both advantages and disadvantages to studying at a foreign university.

MY OPINION I think everyone should do it.

3

INTRODUCTION

TASK PARAPHRASE In many schools, uniforms are mandatory for the students in order to help them concentrate on their schoolwork better.

MY OPINION This is an ineffective practice.

MY THESIS STATEMENT

Main Idea 1 Schools believe that if students don't have a choice about their clothes, they will think more about their studies.

Main Idea 2 Students will always use their clothes for self expression.

Main Idea 3 Students will always find a way to compete with each other socially.

BODY 1

MAIN IDEA 1 If students don't have a choice about their clothes, they will think more about their studies.

Supporting Detail 1 They will be more interested in their class work.

Supporting Detail 2 They won't worry about dressing fashionably.

Supporting Detail 3 I disagree with this.

BODY 2

MAIN IDEA 2 Students will always use their clothes for self expression.

Supporting Detail 1 They can wear their skirts longer or shorter.

Supporting Detail 2 They can tie their ties in different ways.

Supporting Detail 3 They can roll their socks up or down.

BODY 3

MAIN IDEA 3 Students will always find a way to compete with each other socially.

Supporting Detail 1 Making fashions out of uniforms is a way to do this.

Supporting Detail 2 Showing interest in certain types of music or movies is another way.

Supporting Detail 3 Choosing certain types of friends is another way.

CONCLUSION

TASK PARAPHRASE Schools often try to help students focus on academics by requiring uniforms.

MY OPINION However, in most cases this won't work. Uniforms won't change natural behavior.

4

INTRODUCTION

TASK PARAPHRASE Some people believe it is cruel to keep wild animals in zoos and therefore zoos should be prohibited.

MY OPINION I feel that zoos actually benefit wild animals.

MY THESIS STATEMENT **Main Idea 1** Zoos help scientists do better research.

Main Idea 2 With better research we can do more to help wild animals.

Main Idea 3 Zoos are a great way to educate the public.

BODY 1

MAIN IDEA 1 Zoos help scientists do better research.

Supporting Detail 1 They can observe animals more closely.

Supporting Detail 2 They can set up experiments.

Supporting Detail 3 They can control the research environment.

BODY 2

MAIN IDEA 2 With better research we can do more to help wild animals.

Supporting Detail 1 We learn about how animals live and survive.

Supporting Detail 2 Then we can do more to protect their habitat.

Supporting Detail 3 We can do more to stop harmful human activity.

BODY 3

MAIN IDEA 3 Zoos are a great way to educate the public.

Supporting Detail 1 People become interested in wild animals.

Supporting Detail 2 They learn about wild animals and environmental issues.

Supporting Detail 3 They learn about the effects of human activity.

CONCLUSION

TASK PARAPHRASE Zoos are not cruel places.

MY OPINION Zoos help us gain knowledge that benefits wild animals.

5

INTRODUCTION

TASK PARAPHRASE: Many people nowadays buy food that has been prepared at restaurants and grocery stores rather than cooking at home.

MY OPINION: I believe this is a result of the busy lives people lead. I think it is a good thing.

MY THESIS STATEMENT
- **Main Idea 1** People lead busy lives.
- **Main Idea 2** People have more time to spend on important activities.
- **Main Idea 3** People can still eat good food.

BODY 1

MAIN IDEA 1 People lead busy lives.
- **Supporting Detail 1** They work hard at their jobs.
- **Supporting Detail 2** Then they want to relax with family and friends.
- **Supporting Detail 3** They spend time on sports, hobbies, and classes.

BODY 2

MAIN IDEA 2 People have more time to spend on important activities.
- **Supporting Detail 1** They don't have to plan meals, shop, and cook.
- **Supporting Detail 2** They can just buy a meal and eat it.
- **Supporting Detail 3** They can spend their time as they like.

BODY 3

MAIN IDEA 3 People can still eat good food.
- **Supporting Detail 1** People often eat snack food when they are in a hurry.
- **Supporting Detail 2** Snack food is not nutritious and doesn't satisfy.
- **Supporting Detail 3** A prepared meal is delicious and nutritious.

CONCLUSION

TASK PARAPHRASE: Buying prepared meals has become common in the modern world.

MY OPINION: Prepared meals give people time to pursue activities of interest to them.

Write Your Essay

Possible answers

1

People should not have to stop working at any specific age. In my opinion this is unfair and unnecessary. Some people enjoy working, some people need to keep earning money, and everybody needs to feel a purpose in life.

Some people look forward to the day they can quit working, but others enjoy their jobs. They may like the kind of work they do. They may also enjoy interacting with their colleagues. And they may like to feel that they are part of something, such as their company or their profession. It isn't fair to take these things away from them just because they reach a certain age.

Some people need to keep earning money no matter how old they are. If they don't have savings or a pension, then they depend on their salaries to pay their bills. Or, they may have these things but they don't provide enough money to cover all their expenses. Furthermore, people often have more medical needs as they grow older and they need money for these expenses.

Everybody, no matter what age, needs to feel a purpose in life. A job can give this sense of purpose. It can make a person feel useful. It can make a person feel like she is contributing something to the world.

Everybody is different and has different needs. Some people want to stop working at a certain time while others want to work longer. For these reasons, I don't think it is right to make everyone retire at the same age.

2

There are both benefits and drawbacks to studying abroad. I feel that going to a university in a foreign country can be a valuable experience. Although it may make starting a career at home a little difficult, it allows students to learn about another language and culture and also provides educational opportunities they may not have at home.

After returning from studying abroad, a student may have a hard time starting a career at first. This is the main disadvantage of studying abroad. The student may not have had the same kind of training that is required in her country for her career. Also she probably hasn't had the opportunity to make professional connections in her own country. However, with a little time and patience, these disadvantages are easy to overcome.

A big advantage of studying abroad is the opportunity to learn about another language and culture. Foreign language skills are very important for anybody to have, and studying abroad is the best way to develop these skills. Understanding another culture is also very important in today's global economy. This type of knowledge is a big advantage to have when looking for a job.

Sometimes people study abroad because they are looking for a better education. Their own country might not have good universities. Or another may have the best training available in a certain profession. Or the type of training they want may not be available at all where they live.

While there are some disadvantages to studying at a foreign university, the advantages are greater. I think everyone should do it.

3

In many schools, uniforms are mandatory for the students in order to help them concentrate on their schoolwork better. I think this is an ineffective practice. Schools believe that if students don't have a choice about their clothes, they will think more about their studies, but students will always find a way to express themselves through their clothing and they will always find a way to compete with each other socially.

According to some schools, if students all wear the same uniform, they will think about their schoolwork and not about their clothes. They will be more interested in doing well in class. They won't spend time worrying about dressing fashionably. I disagree with this point of view.

I believe that students will always use their clothes for self expression, even if those clothes are a uniform. Students can wear their skirts longer or shorter. They can tie their ties in different ways. They can roll their socks up or down. There are many ways to create fashions with uniforms by making small changes.

It is natural for students, especially high school students, to find ways to compete with each other socially. Making fashions out of uniforms is one way to do this. Showing interest in certain types of music or movies is another way. Choosing certain types of friends is yet another. Wearing uniforms will not stop students from being concerned about their social lives.

Schools often try to help students focus on academics by requiring uniforms. However, in most cases this won't work. Uniforms won't change natural behavior.

4

Some people believe it is cruel to keep wild animals in zoos and therefore zoos should be prohibited. I completely disagree with this opinion because I feel that zoos actually benefit wild animals. Zoos help scientists do better research, and with better research we can do more to help wild animals. Additionally, zoos are a great way to educate the public.

In zoos, scientists can do research that they can't do in the wild. They can observe animals more closely in order to better understand their habits. They can set up experiments to see how animals respond to different situations. They can control the research environment in ways they can't do in the wild.

Better research helps us understand and help wild animals more. It helps us learn more about how animals live and what they need to survive. With this knowledge, we can do more to protect the habitat of wild animals. We can do more to stop human activity that harms them.

Zoos are important because they educate the pubic about animals. By going to zoos, people can develop an interest in wild animals. They can learn about wild animals and environmental issues. They can learn about the effects of human activity on the natural environment.

Zoos are not cruel places. In most zoos, animals are well cared for. The knowledge that we gain by studying animals in zoos can be a big benefit for wild animals. It helps us learn to take better care of them and the natural environment that they live in.

5

Many people nowadays buy food that has been prepared at restaurants and grocery stores rather than cooking at home. I believe this is a result of the busy lives people lead. I think it is a good thing because it means people have more time for activities that are important to them, but they still can eat good food.

Modern people lead busy lives. They work hard at their jobs all day long. In their free time, they want to relax with their family and friends. They also want to pursue activities such as sports or hobbies. Many people also like to take classes to improve their professional knowledge or just to learn something new.

By buying prepared meals, people have more time to spend on the activities that are important to them. They don't have to plan and shop and cook. They can just pick up a meal at a store or restaurant and eat it. Then the rest of their time is free to spend as they like: relaxing, playing with their children, learning something new, or anything else they enjoy.

When people buy prepared meals, they eat good food and get the nutrition they need. People often eat things like potato chips or other snack food when they are in a hurry. This type of food has no nutrition and doesn't really satisfy hunger. A prepared meal, on the other hand, usually includes a variety of delicious and nutritious food. It is a much more healthful way to eat.

Buying prepared meals has become common in the modern world. These days people just don't have time to cook. Eating prepared meals means they can pursue all their activities and eat well at the same time.

Speaking Module

PART 1

PRACTICE 1

Family

Question 1
1. large, older, younger
2. small, uncles, cousins, large
3. wife, parents, relatives, close
4. twin, quiet, distant

Question 2
1. sports, visit, meal
2. read, discussing, opinions, strange
3. vacation, rent, invite
4. busy, cooks, talk, relaxing

Question 3
1. fun, share, interests
2. baby, attention, husband, fine
3. activities, in common
4. groups, like, get along

Food

Question 1
1. trying, dishes, foreign, different
2. meals, traditional, delicious, well
3. vegetarian, prepared, fresh, fruit
4. chicken, rice, desserts, sweet, vegetables

Question 2
1. out, lunch, cafeteria, sandwich
2. breakfast, dinner, weekends
3. expensive, have, special occasion
4. convenient, neighborhood, tastes

Question 3
1. serves, cakes, snack, frequently
2. elegant, birthday, prices
3. fast food, hamburger, quickly, cheap
4. seafood, fish, menu

Hometown

Question 1
1. small, quiet, peaceful, exciting, population
2. large, busy, crowded, interesting
3. mountains, scenery, tourists, medium, fills
4. suburb, pretty, work, entertainment

Question 2
1. world, live, meet
2. attractive, parks, beautiful, famous
3. opportunities, universities, businesses, easy
4. safe, raise, crime

Question 3
1. boring, same, changes
2. traffic, noisy, polluted
3. climate, winters, depressing, prefer, warmer
4. expensive, apartment, bus, afford

School

Question 1
1. graduated, variety, excellent
2. huge, crowded, sports, teams
3. ordinary, usual, activities, basketball, club
4. modern, gym, library, equipment

Question 2
1. biology, science, especially, plants, animals
2. art, talented, drawing
3. Math, definitely, best, challenging
4. history, fascinating, learning, past

Question 3
1. study, pay attention, future, seriously
2. youth, graduate, responsibilities, have fun
3. need, careers, university, prepare
4. subjects, figure out, try out

Transportation

Question 1
1. subways, buses, drive, moves
2. public, cars, train station, long distance
3. take, bicycles, lanes
4. options, taxis, walk, sidewalks

Question 2
1. far, takes, give a ride
2. station, minute, convenient
3. almost, exercise, on time
4. bus stop, transfer

Question 3
1. spend, gasoline, solution, closer
2. fast, fare, rush hour
3. walking, mind, relaxing
4. traffic jams, get, take, drive

Weather

Question 1
1. seasons, depends, varies, warm, cold
2. tropical, hot, rainy, dry, sunny
3. cold, summers, winters, snow
4. pleasant, mild, temperature

Question 2
1. coffee, window, raindrops
2. depressed, dark, cold, hope, change
3. outside, falling, puddles, hard, inside
4. special, care, storm, thunder, scared

Question 3
1. weather, warm, cold, sunshine
2. long, lots, ski, sports
3. offers, Spring, fall, nice, ice
4. rainy, desert, shines, clouds

Exercise

Question 1
1. get, run, keep fit
2. bike, tennis, active
3. work out, favorite, swim, pool
4. yoga, practice, build, strength

Question 2
1. played, teams, competitive, got
2. used to, took, lessons, energy
3. baseball, good at, had
4. particular, ran, jumped

Question 3
1. regularly, enough, lazy
2. health, diet, sick
3. too busy, free time, relax
4. uninteresting, spend, rather

PRACTICE 2

Family

Question 1
Tense markers: When you were younger, did
Answer: (A)

Question 2
Tense markers: In the past, did
Answer: (B)

Question 3
Tense markers: Do
Answer: (B)

Food

Question 1
Tense markers: did, when you were younger
Answer: (B)

Question 2
Tense markers: usually, does
Answer: (A)

Question 3
Tense markers: Did, when you were a child
Answer: (A)

Hometown

Question 1
Tense markers: will, later on
Answer: (B)

Question 2
Tense markers: did, when you were a child
Answer: (B)

Question 3
Tense markers: will, in the future
Answer: (A)

Work

Question 1
Tense markers: did
Answer: (A)

Question 2
Tense markers: do, now
Answer: (B)

Question 3
Tense markers: will, in the future
Answer: (A)

Transportation

Question 1
Tense markers: did, when you were a child
Answer: (B)

Question 2
Tense markers: Will
Answer: (A)

Question 3
Tense markers: Do
Answer: (B)

Weather

Question 1
Tense markers: do
Answer: (A)

Question 2
Tense markers: does
Answer: (A)

Question 3
Tense markers: when you were a child
Answer: (B)

Exercise

Question 1
Tense markers: will, in the future
Answer: (B)

Question 2
Tense markers: do
Answer: (A)

Question 3
Tense markers: did, in the past
Answer: (B)

PART 2

PRACTICE 1

(The Introduction answers are samples only. Many answers are possible.)

2. **Topic:** Talk about a holiday you enjoy celebrating.
   Introduction: The holiday that I most enjoy celebrating is my country's Independence Day.
3. **Topic:** Describe something expensive that you recently bought for yourself.
   Introduction: An expensive thing that I bought recently was a bicycle.
4. **Topic:** Describe a book you enjoyed reading.
   Introduction: A book I enjoyed reading was *Oliver Twist*.
5. **Topic:** Talk about someone who influenced you when you were a child.
   Introduction: My uncle was someone who influenced me when I was a child.

PRACTICE 2

(The notes are samples only. Many answers are possible.)

2

Talk about a holiday you enjoy celebrating.
You should say:
what the name of the holiday is and why people celebrate it
who you usually celebrate it with
what you usually do on this holiday

Notes

what/why: Independence Day; to celebrate the independence of our country
who: my family and neighbors
what: picnic and games in our neighborhood

3

Describe something that you recently bought for yourself.
You should say:
what it is and what it looks like
when you bought it
what you use it for

Notes

what: a racing bicycle; blue, black seat, 12 speeds
when: six months ago
what: ride to school and work

4

Describe a book you enjoyed reading.
You should say:
what the title is and who wrote it
what kind of book it is
what the book is about

Notes

what/who: *Oliver Twist*/Charles Dickens
what kind: novel
what: a poor, innocent orphan boy who gets into a lots of trouble

5

Talk about someone who influenced you when you were a child.
You should say:
who the person was
how you met this person
what things you did together

Notes

who: my Uncle Tom
how: he's part of my family
what: hiking and camping

PRACTICE 3

(These are samples only. Many answers are possible.)

2

Talk about a holiday you enjoy celebrating.
You should say:
what the name of the holiday is and why people celebrate it
who you usually celebrate it with
what you usually do on this holiday
and explain what you enjoy most about it

Notes

spend the day outside
play soccer
eat good food

Talk

The holiday that I most enjoy celebrating is my country's Independence Day. This is the day when we celebrate the independence of our country, of course. I celebrate it with my family, including my cousins and aunts and uncles, and my neighbors. We have a big celebration in my neighborhood. Everybody contributes some food, and we all go to the neighborhood park. We spend the day there cooking and eating and playing all kinds of games. I really like this holiday because it's so much fun to spend the day outside having a good time with my family and neighbors. We always have a big soccer game, and I like that because I love playing soccer. I like picnics, too, because I really love to eat, and the food at our Independence Day celebrations is always so good. I always look forward to this holiday.

3

Describe something that you recently bought for yourself.
You should say:
what it is and what it looks like
when you bought it
what you use it for
and explain why it is important to you to own it

Notes

convenient
no more waiting for the bus
fast

Talk

Something that I bought recently was a bicycle. It's a racing bicycle, even though I don't use it for racing. It's blue with a black seat, and it has twelve speeds. I bought it about six months ago, so I haven't had it for very long. I use it to ride to school and to work. This bike is really important to me because it makes transportation much more convenient. Most days, I have to go to school and then to my job. Before I bought my bicycle, I had to ride the bus at least three times a day. I used to spend a lot of time waiting for buses. Now I don't waste time waiting anymore. I just get on my bicycle and go whenever I'm ready. I can get everywhere much faster than I did before. It makes my life a lot easier.

4

Describe a book you enjoyed reading.
You should say:
what the title is and who wrote it
what type of book it is
what the book is about
and explain why you enjoyed it.

Notes

I like Dickens.
I like the characters.
I like the setting.

Talk

A book I enjoyed reading was *Oliver Twist*. It was written by Charles Dickens, and it's a novel. It's about a poor orphan boy named Oliver Twist. He is an innocent boy, but he always gets into trouble. A rich man finds him and tries to take care of him, but then he ends up living with some thieves. Then the rich man finds him again, so the story has a happy ending. I enjoyed this book because Dickens is one of my favorite authors. I've read several of his books and they are all very interesting. I like the characters in *Oliver Twist*. Some of them are funny and some are sad, but each one has something real. I also like the setting. The story took place in the past, and I like to read about the past. I like to get an idea of what life was like in a different time and place.

5

> Talk about someone who influenced you when you were a child.
> You should say:
> who the person was
> how you met this person
> what things you did together
> and explain how this person influenced you.

Notes

I learned to enjoy the outdoors.
I learned about nature.
He influenced my career choice.

Talk

My Uncle Tom was someone who influenced me when I was a child. I've always known him since he's part of my family. I spent a lot of time with him when I was young. He often took me hiking in the mountains, and sometimes we went camping, too. Uncle Tom taught me to love the outdoors. I still like to go hiking and to spend time outdoors. It's still one of my favorite things to do. My uncle also taught me to love nature. He taught me a lot about plants and animals while we were hiking. Because of that, I've decided to study biology. So I can say he really influenced my career choice.

PART 3

PRACTICE 1

Sample answers (Many answers are possible, these are just samples).

2

opinion: yes, but not just books
reasons/examples: books provide facts and information
there are other sources of information
opinion statement: Most people believe that reading is important because it is how we learn facts and ideas, and I agree. However, I think there are other sources of information besides books.

3

opinion:	learning about new places is better
reasons/examples:	we have other opportunities to relax vacations are the only opportunity to travel to other places
opinion statement:	In my opinion, it's better to use vacation time to visit new places because we have plenty of other opportunities to relax but no other time to travel.

4

opinion:	two important characteristics
reasons/examples:	honesty kindness
opinion statement:	As I see it, the two most important characteristics of a good role model are honesty and kindness.

5

opinion:	yes
reasons/examples:	fewer things to worry about more opportunities for fun
opinion statement:	In my opinion, people who have a lot of money are happier because they have fewer things to worry about and more opportunities to have fun.

PRACTICE 2

Sample answers (Many answers are possible; these are just samples).

2

reasons/examples	supporting details
books	books have limits
other sources	magazines Internet

Talk

Most people believe that reading is important because it is how we learn facts and ideas, and I agree. However, I think there are other sources of information besides books. Books are an important source of information, but they have limits. It takes a long time to write and publish a book, so the information might be out of date. Magazines are another important source of information. Since they are published weekly or monthly, the information in them is newer than the information in books. The Internet has the newest information since things can be published there instantly. I think it is important to read a lot of different things and get information from different kinds of sources.

3

reasons/examples	supporting details
other opportunities to relax	evenings weekends
vacations are the only opportunity to travel	need time it's important to see other places

Talk

In my opinion, it's better to use vacation time to visit new places because we have plenty of other opportunities to relax but no other time to travel. Every evening you can go home after work and relax with your friends and family. On weekends you have two entire days to relax. There's no reason to travel far away just to take a rest. However, evenings and weekends don't give us enough time to travel to other places. We only have enough time for this during vacations. I think everyone should travel to other places when they can. It's important to see what life is like in other countries or even in other parts of your own country. It's important to understand other people. Travel is the best way to do this.

4

reasons/examples	**supporting details**
honesty	don't tell lies show your true self
kindness	help others be nice to others

Talk

As I see it, the two most important characteristics of a good role model are honesty and kindness. A good role model demonstrates honesty. Children need to learn the importance of being truthful and not telling lies. A good role model is also honest about who she is. She isn't afraid to show her true self to others. A good role model is also kind. She helps others who need help. In general, she is nice to other people. Her actions show children how to treat other people with kindness.

5

reasons/examples	**supporting details**
fewer things to worry about	enough money for food, housing, clothes, other needs
more opportunities for fun	pay for entertainment, vacations can pay for friends, too

Talk

In my opinion, people who have a lot of money are happier because they have fewer things to worry about and more opportunities to have fun. People with money are happy because they don't have to worry about paying the rent. They always have enough money for food and to buy clothes for their growing children. They never have to think about how they will pay for the things they need. They also have more opportunities to have fun. They can easily pay for any entertainment they like, such as movies, concerts, or theater tickets. They can go on any kind of vacation they like without wondering if it's too expensive. In addition, they can invite anyone they like to accompany them because they have enough money to pay for their friends, too. So they never have to do anything alone.

PRACTICE 3

Sample answers

2. You're asking me if I think foreign travel is important.
3. If I understand you correctly, you want to know whether people will read less in the future.
4. You'd like me to give some reasons for spending money on certain things.
5. Do you want me to explain why role models are important?

Strategy Review

Part 1

What kind of job do you have?
1. Pay attention to verb tense.
2. Know vocabulary to talk about yourself.
3. Know vocabulary to talk about yourself.

What are your responsibilities at your job?
1. Know vocabulary to talk about yourself.
2. Pay attention to verb tense.
3. Know vocabulary to talk about yourself.
4. Know vocabulary to talk about yourself.
5. Know vocabulary to talk about yourself.

What did you study in order to qualify for this job?
1. Pay attention to verb tense.
2. Pay attention to verb tense.
3. Know vocabulary to talk about yourself.
4. Pay attention to verb tense.

Do you think you will have a different kind of job in the future?
1. Pay attention to verb tense.
2. Pay attention to verb tense.
3. Pay attention to verb tense.
4. Know vocabulary to talk about yourself.

Part 2

1. Introduce your talk.
2. Pay attention to question words.
3. Pay attention to question words.
4. Pay attention to question words.
5. Think of three reasons.
6. Think of three reasons.
7. Think of three reasons.

Part 3

Do you prefer to spend your free time alone or with other people?
1. Introduce your response by stating your opinion.
2. Expand your answer with supporting details.
3. Expand your answer with supporting details.
4. Expand your answer with supporting details.
5. Expand your answer with supporting details.

Do you think people need more free time than they generally have? Why or why not?
1. Introduce your response by stating your opinion.
2. Expand your answer with supporting details.

3. Expand your answer with supporting details.
4. Expand your answer with supporting details.
5. Expand your answer with supporting details.
6. Expand your answer with supporting details.
7. Expand your answer with supporting details.
8. Expand your answer with supporting details.
9. Expand your answer with supporting details.

How are free-time activities now different from the way they were in the past?

1. Introduce your response by stating your opinion.
2. Expand your answer with supporting details.
3. Expand your answer with supporting details.
4. Expand your answer with supporting details.
5. Expand your answer with supporting details.
6. Expand your answer with supporting details.
7. Expand your answer with supporting details.
8. Expand your answer with supporting details.
9. Expand your answer with supporting details.

AUDIOSCRIPTS

Narrator: This CD includes the audio for the Listening and Speaking Modules for IELTS Strategies and TIPS by Lin Lougheed. Copyright 2013 by Lin Lougheed.

Narrator: Key Word Strategies

NARRATOR: EXAMPLE 1

Woman: Our agency has quite a few apartments listed in your price range. So a lot will depend on which part of the city you are interested in.
Man: I'd prefer not to be too far from downtown, or at least close to the subway.

Woman: Well, that gives us several options. You may like Luxury Towers. There are several vacant apartments there now. There is one on the top floor that has a view that's quite spectacular. You can see the harbor very clearly from there.
Man: Great. How big is the apartment?

Woman: All the apartments in the building are quite spacious, and in addition to a large living room, each also has a separate dining room as well as an eat-in kitchen.
Man: I'd definitely like to visit Luxury Towers. But I'd like to look in other buildings, too.

Woman: Parkview Apartments will have some vacancies soon. All the ground floor apartments there have a small patio, which is a very nice feature.
Man: Will any of the ground floor apartments be vacant soon?

Woman: Yes, there will be one available next month. Now, if you'd like to be right downtown, I can show you some apartments on Main Street.
Man: Yes, I'd like to see them.

Woman: They're the smallest apartments I have to show you, but despite that, they're also the most expensive, because of the location, you know.
Man: I think it's still worth looking at.

NARRATOR: EXAMPLE 2

Theory X and Theory Y are theories of motivation in the workplace developed by social psychologist Douglas McGregor in the 1960s. They describe how managers may perceive their employees rather than how employees actually act.

A Theory X manager assumes that workers are not motivated and dislike their jobs. Therefore, they have to be controlled and supervised every step of the way or they will not carry out their duties. They avoid responsibility or taking on any extra work. Workplaces that ascribe to Theory X are hierarchical with many levels of managers and supervisors to keep the workers under control.

Theory Y describes the opposite situation. This theory assumes that employees are self-motivated and enjoy their work, that they want greater responsibility and don't need a lot of supervision. Theory Y managers believe that their employees want to do well at work and that, given the right conditions, they will. In a Theory Y workplace, even lower-level employees are involved in decision making.

Narrator: Practice

Narrator: Passage 1

Welcome to Richland Mansion. We'll begin our tour of the grounds in just a minute. Afterwards you are free to tour the inside of the mansion on your own or join a guided tour. There is one every hour. OK, here we are at the fountain, which Mr. Richland imported from Italy in 1885. If you'll take a look at this map here, I'll show you where the tour will continue. The rose garden is right across the brook from here, and we'll cross this wooden bridge to get to it. Then we'll stroll along the banks of the brook to the guest house, which we will view from the outside, but the inside is not open to visitors. After that, we'll continue along the brook until we come to the stone bridge, here, where we'll cross back over the brook to get to the pine forest, here. It's really just a small forested area. We'll follow a trail that will bring us out on the other side of the forest and then take us up to the mansion. On the way, we can stop and look at the vegetable garden, here, and you'll see that the mansion is just beyond that.

Narrator: Passage 2

Man: So, we've got all the research done. We sure did a lot of interviews! Now we've got to get to work on the report and the class presentation.
Woman: Let's plan the presentation first. We've got to give it next week.

Man: Right. OK, so I thought we could invite one of the people we interviewed to be a guest speaker.
Woman: I don't think the professor would like that at all. The presentation is supposed to be completely by us.

Man: Well, maybe you're right. OK, so we won't do that, but we should show some charts and graphs.
Woman: Agreed. That's the best way to explain the data we gathered. I can prepare those. What about photographs? You took a lot when we were going around interviewing people.

Man: Yes, but I want to look through them to see if there are any good ones.
Woman: OK, so if there are some good ones, maybe we'll show them. I was thinking maybe we should pass out transcripts of some of the interviews we did.

Man: I don't think so. That's way too much. I think we should just summarize that information orally. But we definitely should pass out copies of the questionnaire.
Woman: Definitely. They'll want to see exactly what questions we asked in the interviews.

Narrator: Passage 3

Single stream recycling is a system of collecting recyclables from residences that is gaining increased attention from around the country. Traditionally, households have had to sort their recyclables into different bins according to material—paper, glass, plastic—for pickup by city trucks. In single stream recycling, all the materials go into one bin. They are later sorted at a recycling facility. One of the major benefits of this system is that, because it is so simple, more people are likely to recycle their waste instead of putting it in the trash. On the other hand, some cities that have implemented this system have been receiving phone calls from furious residents who don't understand how the system works. They continue to sort their recyclables and can't see why everything is thrown together into one truck. So clearly, some education is needed. Another attraction for cities using this system is the low cost of pickup. Since all recyclables can be mixed together in one truck, multiple trips to each neighborhood are not necessary. On the downside, there are high start-up costs, not only for initial purchase of the trucks but also for the construction of the processing plant where the recyclables are sorted. In addition, processing recyclables under this system can be more expensive than under older systems.

Narrator: Passage 4

Man: Good afternoon. Piano Rentals Unlimited. How may I help you?
Woman: Yes. Thank you. I'd like to rent a piano for my daughter. She's interested in learning to play.

Man: All right. We certainly can help you with that. I'll just need to take some information first. Your name?
Woman: Patricia Gable.

Man: Gable? Could you spell that please?
Woman: G-A-B-L-E.

Man: B-L-E. Thanks. And what's your address?
Woman: 13 Main Street.

Man: 13 Main Street. Got it. What type of piano were you looking to rent?
Woman: Oh, just an upright piano, one that would fit in our living room. We don't have a whole lot of space.

Man: I think we can find something to suit you. Now, did you want it right away.
Woman: No, my daughter won't be starting lessons until the beginning of next month, so we won't need it until then.

Man: I can have it delivered to you on June first. Will that do?
Woman: Perfect. I don't know how long your rentals usually are, but I was hoping we could have it for six months.

Man: Six months will be fine. I'll make a note of that. Now, did you want to pay today with a credit card, or will you send us a check?
Woman: I'll pay now. Just let me find my credit card so I can give you the number.

Narrator: Passage 5

Good evening. Welcome to the Riverdale Cyclists Club meeting. Before we show the slides from last month's trip, I'm going to go over a few things you should know for next month's upcoming trip to the White River Valley. I believe most of you in the audience are planning to participate in that trip. So, the first question I'm always asked is: What should I bring from home? The number one item you should bring on this trip is your own bike. Don't laugh. On many of our trips it's possible to rent bikes, but unfortunately there will be no rentals available on the White River Valley trip. However, the tour company will be providing each one of you with your own personalized water bottle, so that's one thing you won't have to pack. And maps, of course. We'll have several experienced guides who know the area well, so maps and guide books won't be needed. While all meals will be provided, you'll probably want to bring along some snacks to help keep your energy up on the road, so don't forget that. And it's quite sunny in that part of the country, so a protective sun hat is also a good idea. We'll be spending nights at different hotels along the way, so no camping equipment will be necessary. The area we'll be biking through is very scenic and I'm sure most of you will want to take photographs, so bring along any photographic equipment you want.

NARRATOR: LISTENING MODULE

General Strategies

NARRATOR: PRACTICE 1

Narrator: Audio 1

Woman: A room for two people is two hundred fifty dollars a night.
Man: That seems a bit high.

Woman: The rooms are very comfortable. And we serve complimentary breakfast to all our guests every morning from seven to nine.
Man: That sounds nice. Do you have an exercise room?

Woman: No, but there is a club across the street you can use, for a small fee. We do have our own pool, which guests can use free of charge.
Man: Oh, that's good. I'll certainly use that. Do you serve other meals besides breakfast?

Woman: Yes, we serve three meals a day, plus afternoon tea. The menu and price list are available on our website if you'd like to see them.
Man: Oh, OK. I'll take a look at it.

Woman: You might also like to know that each room has a large screen TV, and for an extra fee you can order movies.

Narrator: Audio 2

Welcome to Urban Tours. We'll begin our tour today with a bus ride through City Park, which is known for its landscaping and gardens. We'll spend an hour walking through the park's Central Flower garden, which is in full bloom this time of year. Then we'll get back on the bus and ride over the White River Bridge and on to the history museum. Before visiting the museum, we'll enjoy lunch at Shell's Café, located just one block away, and then take a brief walk through the neighborhood to view some historic buildings. Then we'll enjoy a special guided tour of the museum, and we'll have an hour or two after that to visit the nearby shopping district where you can make any purchases you want before returning to the hotel.

Track 7

Narrator: Audio 3

Man: I have a really tough schedule this semester.
Woman: You're taking some difficult classes, aren't you?

Man: It's not that so much, but I think I chose the wrong courses. My chemistry class, for example, has way too many students in it.
Woman: Really?

Man: Yeah. It's impossible to ask a question or get any attention from the instructor because of that.
Woman: What about your math class? You were really looking forward to taking that.

Man: I was, but, like I said, I chose the wrong class. I never knew math could be so boring.
Woman: That's too bad. So I guess you feel like this semester is a complete waste.

Man: Actually, no. Believe it or not, I'm really enjoying my psychology class. I like it the best of all my classes.

Narrator: Audio 4

Although rabbits and hares are very similar in appearance, they are different animals with different characteristics. We can say that the differences start at birth. Baby hares are able to defend themselves, at least to some degree, because they can see when they are born. When rabbits are born, however, they cannot see and so are completely helpless. Unlike hares, rabbits stick together, living with other rabbits in colonies. They live in underground burrows, which provide a safe place to hide from predators. Hares, on the other hand, live most of their lives as loners. They stay above the ground and are able to avoid predators because they are such good runners. Hares and rabbits also have different eating habits. Hares tend to favor bark, twigs, and other woody plants, while rabbits prefer softer grasses, leaves, and stems.

NARRATOR: PRACTICE 2

1. The project will start on April first two thousand sixteen.
2. Each ticket costs fifteen dollars and fifty cents.
3. A meal costs ten seventy-five.
4. The program begins at half past six.
5. My phone number is five five five six three seven one two oh four.
6. My credit card number is two zero eight four three seven nine nine.
7. I started working here on June seventh, twenty-ten.
8. I live at two thirty-one Main Street.
9. The bus will depart at a quarter past nine.

10. The bus fare is three forty-five per person.
11. The phone number is three oh one two three four thirteen twenty-five.
12. My membership number is six five seven double three eight one.
13. The course fee is six hundred eighty dollars.
14. The class begins at ten forty-five.
15. My home address is seventeen oh six Maple Avenue.

Narrator: Section 1

Narrator: Practice 1

Narrator: Conversation 1

Woman: Good morning. Argyle Car Rentals. How may I help you?
Man: Yes. Thank you. I'd like to find out about renting a car.

Woman: Certainly. Just let me take some information first. May I have your name?
Man: William Harville.

Woman: Harville. That's h-a-r-v…?
Man: h-a-r-v-i-double l-e

Woman: double l-e. Got it. And may I have your address?
Man: 17 North Cameron Street, Compton.

Woman: Thank you. Do you have a valid driver's license?
Man: Yes, of course.

Woman: I'll need to know the number, then.
Man: Oh, certainly. It's five zero three six seven three one.

Woman: … six seven three one. Right. OK. Are you insured? We require automobile insurance.
Man: Yes. I'm insured with Green Brothers.

Woman: Green Brothers, great. Most of our customers are with them, though some go with Sillington Insurance.
Man: Well, I'm with Green. Um, OK, so I'm going to need a somewhat large car, so I'm hoping you've got something that's not compact.

Woman: We have a range of choices. You might want to go with a mid-size sedan.
Man: No, larger.

Woman: A small truck? A van?
Man: Not a truck. I think a van will do.

Woman: Fine. I'll put you down for that. What date did you want to pick it up?
Man: December twelfth. Is that possible?

Woman: Of course. Will you be paying by credit card?
Man: Yes.

Narrator: Conversation 2

Man: Crystal Theater Box Office.
Woman: Good Morning. This is Petronella Jones speaking. I'd like to order some tickets for your current show.

Man: *Romeo and Juliet*. Yes. We still have seats available. What date were you interested in?
Woman: I was hoping to go next Friday.

Man: I'm sorry, but Friday is sold out. We do have some seats available for Saturday evening, and for both Sunday afternoon and evening.
Woman: Hmmm. I think it'll have to be Sunday.

Man: OK, that's March tenth. Which show are you interested in? Show times are three o'clock and seven thirty.
Woman: Put me down for the earlier one.

Man: Three o'clock, then. How many tickets would you like?
Woman: It'll just be me and my husband.

Man: So, that would be two. Fine. Now what part of the theater would you like to sit in? We still have several boxes available.
Woman: I think a box would be too expensive.

Man: Well, there are orchestra seats, or the other location would be the balcony.
Woman: We'll take the balcony. What's the price?

Man: That depends. You might be eligible for a discount. Patrons over age sixty, for example, can get a senior citizen discount.
Woman: Put me down for that.

Man: Fine. I'll make a note of it. Will you be picking up the tickets, or shall I mail them to you?
Woman: Mail them, please.

Narrator: Conversation 3

Man: Sanditon Hotel. May I help you?
Woman: Yes, I'd like to reserve a room for next week. Do you have any available?

Man: We do. Just let me take your information. Name?
Woman: Cathy Wiggins.

Man: Is that Cathy with a K or a C?
Woman: With a C. C-a-t-h-y.

Man: And what date do you plan to arrive?
Woman: June twenty-third. That's a Friday. I was planning to stay the entire weekend, Friday, Saturday, Sunday.

Man: Three nights, then. Fine. We have several rooms available for those nights. What type of room did you want? I have several singles and doubles open, and I have some suites available, too.
Woman: A suite would be very nice; however, I'm traveling alone, so I think I'll just need a single room.

Man: Fine. There are several to choose from. I have one looking out over the park and another with a view of the ocean.
Woman: Oh, the ocean. I definitely want to see the ocean from my room.

Man: I'll put you in room number 34 then. Now, I'll just need your credit card number.
Woman: It's four seven nine two eight five four.

Man: Four seven nine two eight five four. Thank you.

Narrator: Conversation 4

Woman: Good afternoon. Westfield Language Academy.
Man: Good afternoon. I'm interested in signing up for some French classes.

Woman: Perfect. We have new classes beginning next week. Just let me get some information from you. I'll need your name and address.
Man: My name is Ronald McGraw and I live at three fifty-one Bond Street.

Woman: Is that Bond with a B?
Man: Yes. B-o-n-d.

Woman: Perfect. If you would just give me your phone number.
Man: Four three six five eight oh one.

Woman: Five eight oh one. OK. You said you were interested in French classes. Have you ever studied French before?
Man: Yes, but only a little.

Woman: Then you probably wouldn't want to take an advanced class. What about intermediate?
Man: I think I would be more comfortable with a beginning level class.

Woman: Then I'll sign you up for Beginning French. We have two of those courses starting next week. One is on Monday and Wednesday evenings and the other is on Tuesday and Thursday afternoons.
Man: It'll have to be the first one because I'm not free in the afternoons.

Woman: Perfect. OK, the course costs five hundred dollars for four weeks. You can pay now by credit card, or would you prefer to mail us a check.
Man: I think I'll send a check.

Woman: All right. We'll need to receive it before Friday in order to hold your place in the class.
Man: I'll send it this afternoon.

Narrator: Conversation 5

Woman: Hello. I'm a student here at the university, and I'm looking for a job.
Man: Then you've called the right place. I'd be happy to help you. First, could I have your name and address, please?

Woman: Oh. Yes. My name is Shirley Chang. My address is PO Box two seventy-five Bradford.
Man: Box two seventy-five Bradford. OK. Next, I'll need to know when you're available to start work.

Woman: Well, I guess as soon as possible. How about the first of next month? That's very soon.
Man: That sounds fine. I'll put you down for September first. Now, what type of job are you looking for? I'm guessing you're not looking for a full-time job.

Woman: No. I'm a student, so I can only work part-time.
Man: That's just fine. We have a lot of part-time listings. What can you tell me about your previous work experience?

Woman: Well, I've never worked, so I guess I have none.
Man: I'll just put down none, then. That's not a problem. Most of our jobs are entry level. What about skills? Do you speak any other languages? Spanish? Chinese?

Woman: Unfortunately, no. But I know a lot about computers. I have good computer skills.
Man: Excellent. I think we have several job listings that would be suitable for you.

NARRATOR: PRACTICE 2

Narrator: Conversation 1

Woman: Could you tell me the schedule for the Spanish classes?
Man: Yes. It depends on the level. We don't have any Beginning Spanish courses this term. We do have an Intermediate Spanish class that meets two afternoons a week, Monday and Wednesday from one to three.

Woman: And how much does it cost?
Man: The four-week course is just five hundred seventy-five dollars. That's a class for adults only. You must be over eighteen to take it.

Woman: Yes, naturally. What about advanced Spanish? When does that meet?
Man: That's just one afternoon a week, on Tuesday. It's fewer hours, so a four-week course costs only four hundred fifty dollars.

Woman: Do you have any classes for children?
Man: Beginning Chinese is for children ages ten to fourteen. It meets on Saturday.

Woman: I meant for younger children.
Man: We have a Beginning French class that meets Wednesday and Friday for children ages six to ten.

Woman: And what's the cost?
Man: All our children's classes cost three hundred twenty-five dollars.

Narrator: Conversation 2

Woman: I've been looking over the August calendar for the Arts Center. There are a number of interesting events coming up.
Man: I know. I definitely want to attend the film festival on August tenth. It's all day from ten in the morning till eight at night. I think that's a great deal for just thirty-five dollars.

Woman: And it's taking place in the new Circle Theater. I hear it's very nice. Oh, and the next day, on the eleventh is another all-day event from nine to five. A crafts fair.
Man: You can go if you like. I think I'll skip that one.

Woman: I don't mind. I see it's being held in the main lobby, so I don't imagine it will be very large. That lobby doesn't have a lot of space.
Man: Hmm, yes. I definitely don't want to miss this event on the seventeenth in the Starlight Theater—*Romeo and Juliet*.

Woman: Oh, I want to see that, too. Although forty-two dollars for the tickets does seem a bit steep.
Man: I'm sure it'll be worth it. What do you think about this afternoon event on August twenty-fourth? A three o'clock concert in Rigby Hall.

Woman: I think that sounds nice. It's been a while since I've heard good music.
Man: I'll order the tickets, then. Eighteen dollars, not bad.

Narrator: Conversation 3

Woman: What are you looking for on the Internet?
Man: I'm checking the online employment listings. I need a job but the problem is I can only work part time because I'm taking a full load of classes this semester.

Woman: But it looks like a lot of these listings are for part-time jobs. Look, here's one at that restaurant on Maple Street.
Man: I can't see working at a restaurant. I don't want to be a waiter.

Woman: Keep reading. It's a job for a manager. It starts October 15. Hey, that's next week. And the pay's 18 dollars an hour. Not bad.
Man: Hmm, maybe. But I can't start that soon. I'll be away visiting my family until the 19th.

Woman: Well, here's a clothing store looking for a bookkeeper. It doesn't start until October 22.
Man: And they pay 21 dollars an hour. I could live with that! Oh, here's a hotel that needs a receptionist to start October 23. That might be kind of fun.

Woman: But, they're only paying 15 dollars an hour.
Man: I need to earn more than that.

Woman: Then I suppose you wouldn't want to apply for this job: administrative assistant at a law office. I can't believe they're only paying 13 dollars an hour.
Man: I'm definitely not interested in that. I think I might try for that job in the clothing store, though. I know a little bit about bookkeeping.

Narrator: Conversation 4

Woman: I need to rent a car for the week I'll be in Miami, but I can't decide what to get.
Man: Let's check out Argyle's website. They've usually got good prices. [Pause, sound of computer keys] See? They charge only 35 dollars a day for a compact car. Oh, and this is cool—all their compact cars are equipped with a roof rack for carrying extra bags, just in case you've got a lot of luggage.

Woman: That sounds good, but how many passengers can one of those cars hold?
Man: Let's see. It says here that there's room for up to four passengers to ride comfortably.

Woman: I'm afraid that isn't large enough.
Man: They have mid-size cars that can carry five passengers comfortably. But they cost 50 dollars a day.

Woman: Yes, but I see you get a sunroof with that size car. Nice. The only problem is, I'll be traveling with a group of six people.
Man: Maybe you should rent a van. It looks like their vans can carry eight passengers, but you have to pay 75 dollars a day to rent one.

Woman: Well, if I want a bigger car, I guess I'll have to pay for it. I wonder if the vans have sun roofs, too.
Man: It doesn't look like they do. But they do have DVD players.

Woman: The van definitely sounds good. But maybe a small truck would be better.
Man: I don't think so, because it says here they can carry no more than four passengers at a time. You could rent two, but that would get expensive since it would cost you 85 dollars a day each. Of course, you might want the truck if you plan to go camping.

Woman: Why is that?
Man: Because, look, it says here that the seats fold down to form a large bed. It sounds more comfortable than sleeping in a tent.

Woman: I think I'll take the van.

Narrator: Conversation 5

Woman: Have you seen this brochure? There are a number of interesting tours we can take while visiting the city.
Man: I know. I really want to view the paintings in the art museum. It's only a two-hour tour, so that would leave plenty of time to do other things the rest of the day.

Woman: And I see we would take the subway to get to the museum. That's convenient. What about this tour of the National Park?
Man: I'm not sure. It's a hike and it lasts four hours. Just the thought of it makes me feel tired.

Woman: But you get to ride back to the hotel afterwards on the bus.
Man: No, I don't think I want to do that tour. But if you want to walk, what about this tour of downtown? We would get to visit all the monuments, and it's only three hours of city walking. That sounds a little easier than the four-hour hike.

Woman: OK, I'll do that one with you if you promise to go to Grover Mansion with me.
Man: Do I have to?

Woman: Oh, come on. It's just a two-hour house tour. You'll love it. And it looks like we'll be getting there by taxi, so you don't have to worry about crowded subways or walking far or anything like that.
Man: Oh, OK. Put it on our schedule.

NARRATOR: PRACTICE 3

Narrator: Conversation 1

Man: I'm looking forward to the French class I'll be taking at the language academy. I was wondering if you offer any activities outside of class. I know some language schools teach students how to prepare meals, for example, as a sort of cultural activity.

Woman: I'm afraid we don't have anything like that specifically, but we do offer a number of other activities. For example, there's usually a party every Saturday evening, and you are only allowed to speak the language you are studying at the party.

Man: That sounds challenging, but a good way to learn. What about foreign language films?
Woman: Oh, yes, we have quite a good series of both French and Spanish films, and we also hope to show some Chinese films soon. You can find the schedule on our website.

Man: I really enjoy sports. I especially like to play soccer. Does the academy have any teams? Or any organized hikes, or any other outdoor activities?
Woman: I'm afraid we're too small to put together anything like that.

Man: Too bad. I have just one more question. Where can I buy the books for my French class?
Woman: At the Academy Bookstore, just across the hall.

Narrator: Conversation 2

Man: I'd really like to hear about your homestay experience since I'd like to try a homestay, too. What was it like living with a Chinese family? I bet you got to travel a lot.
Woman: Actually, my family didn't take any trips while I was staying with them. But that's OK. I really enjoyed being at home with them and having the opportunity to practice my Chinese.

Man: Yes, that's the best way to learn to speak a foreign language, isn't it? You probably met a lot of people during your homestay, didn't you?
Woman: Well, that's the funny part of it. I actually didn't meet a lot of new people. The family I stayed with just wasn't that way. But I'll tell you something they did like to do. Eat. They ate a lot. I ate a lot of different Chinese dishes that I'd never tried before. It was great.

Man: That makes me really want to try a homestay. I'm going to sign up for one as soon as I return from my holiday.

Narrator: Conversation 3

Woman: Have you made your summer plans yet, Lee?
Man: I'm working on them. The first thing I'll do, as soon as I'm finished with my classes, is go spend some time with my family.

Woman: You haven't seen your parents in a while, have you?
Man: Not since the beginning of the semester. I'll probably see some of my cousins, too.

Woman: Will you come back here after that to take any summer classes? That's what I plan to do.
Man: Oh, no. I need a break from studying.

Woman: Then you must be planning to just relax all summer.
Man: Not exactly. I actually have a big trip planned. I'm going to take a long hike through the northern mountains. I'm really looking forward to it.

Woman: You're crazy! That sounds difficult. And dangerous. Have you ever done anything like that before?
Man: Just a little bit. But I've read quite a lot about it, so I think I'm fairly well prepared for it. And I'm going with some friends who have a lot of experience.

Woman: Well, good luck!

Narrator: Conversation 4

Man: I noticed that the monthly fee for these condominiums is quite high. What services, exactly, are covered by the fee?
Woman: Oh, the usual things. All the outside is taken care of, you know, they cut the grass, trim the bushes, keep the gardens nice, that sort of thing.

Man: Good, good. What about parking? The fee includes a space in the garage, doesn't it?
Woman: Actually, no. You can park your car in the outdoor lot, of course, but if you want a space in the garage, you have to pay extra.

Man: That's a disappointment. Hmmmm. Well, what about repairs to the individual apartments?
Woman: Maintenance of the outside of the buildings is included, of course, but each owner is responsible for repairs to his or her own apartment.

Man: Well, I guess that makes sense. I actually don't mind doing a little work around my own apartment. At least it gives me the chance to get some exercise.
Woman: I know what you mean.

Man: It sounds like there's a lot the condo fee doesn't include. Is there anything else that it does cover?
Woman: There's the weekly garbage pick up. The condo fee pays for that.

Man: Well, at least that's something.

Narrator: Conversation 5

Man: I'm applying for a job here and I wonder if you could tell me a little bit about what the work is like.
Woman: Oh, sure. It's a great place to work.

Man: Really?
Woman: Yes. Everyone on the staff is really nice. They're all very helpful to new employees.

Man: That's good to know.
Woman: It's a good place for a student like yourself to work. You probably don't have a lot of experience, right?

Man: Right.
Woman: But you get good training here and everyone is patient while you're learning.

Man: Well, I'm glad to hear that.
Woman: Yes, and the manager is talking about raising our pay next month. It's already pretty good. I mean, this job pays at least as well as other similar jobs, and now they want to give us a raise.

Man: It sounds like they know how to treat their employees well.
Woman: They do. Really, the only problem I have with this job is that it's so far from my house. I wish it were in another place. But it's good for you since it's so near the university.

Man: Yes, that's the main reason I applied to work here.
Woman: OK. Well, I guess they'll be giving you your schedule soon. I look forward to working with you.

Narrator: Section 2

NARRATOR: PRACTICE 1

Narrator: Talk 1

Welcome to the Tapei 101 building. At 509 meters, it is the tallest building in Taiwan and also one of the tallest in the world. Construction of this skyscraper took five years, beginning in 1999. It was completed in 2004. The structure's 101 aboveground stories are occupied by stores, offices, and restaurants, including a shopping mall that takes up six floors. In addition, there are five stories below the ground. In a minute, we will use the elevators to travel to an observation deck near the top of the building. These are the fastest in the world.

Narrator: Talk 2

Washington, DC is a city of monuments. In fact, they are among the most popular tourist attractions in the city. We will be visiting several of them on our bus tour today, and we will go inside one of the most famous of them all, the Washington Monument. It is the tallest structure in the city, but by no means the oldest. That honor goes to the Stone House, in the Georgetown neighborhood, which we will also visit. We have lovely sunny weather for our tour today. As we ride by the river, we may see crowds of office workers as they enjoy their lunch outside. The park by the river is a popular lunchtime spot on nice days such as this.

Narrator: Talk 3

Welcome to Central Park, one of New York City's most famous landmarks. Central Park covers an area of eight hundred forty-three acres in the middle of Manhattan. Aside from being an area of natural beauty, the park offers many recreation opportunities for local residents and visitors alike. You will find several lakes and ponds in the park. Additionally, there are two skating rinks for wintertime skating. During the summer months of July and August, one of these is converted into a swimming pool.

A large reservoir covers one hundred six acres near the middle of the park. In the early mornings, especially, you will find large numbers of runners on the path that encircles the reservoir. It certainly is a scenic place to get your daily exercise! Additionally, the six miles of roads throughout the park are enjoyed by walkers, joggers, cyclists, and horseback riders. They are particularly crowded on weekends, when automobile traffic is prohibited.

Narrator: Talk 4

Good morning, and thank you for coming out today to tour Green Acres, the city's newest residential community. Green Acres includes a mix of apartments and single-family homes and was built for the families of the twenty-first century. Although quite large, the community took just over two years to complete. Work on the first building began in early 2010, and the last nail was driven well before the end of 2012. You'll see on this map here that the hub of the community is this large shopping complex, containing a variety of stores as well as banks, a post office, and other services. Just over here, almost right next to the complex, are the apartment buildings. So shopping and errands are quite convenient for the residents living there. Down here is the Community Center building, which has a variety of programs for both adults and children. There are different kinds of classes, organized trips, and even an indoor tennis court. The community center has a particularly good sports program for children, and on most days you can see a kids soccer game going on in the field just in back of the center. OK, I think that's enough of an introduction. Let's begin our tour.

Narrator: Talk 5

Welcome to Grover Mansion. Let me give you a bit of information before we begin our tour. Now, it may be hard to imagine when you look at the building today, but, in fact, its original purpose was not a residence. The building was originally constructed to house a small clothing factory, and that continued to be its purpose for about fifty years until it was bought by the Grover family in 1910 and converted into a family home. We'll begin our tour in the basement. Don't expect to see a furnace or storage space, such as you would find in a modern house. Instead, that part of the house contains the kitchen, which is how most houses were designed at that time. From there, we'll continue to the ground floor. Of particular interest there is the back porch, a large and spacious area which is now furnished with chairs and coffee tables but which the Grover family usually used as a sleeping place on hot summer evenings.

NARRATOR: PRACTICE 2

Narrator: Talk 1

Good afternoon and welcome to the City Museum of History. We're starting our tour right here in the lobby by the main entrance. This room itself is of historical interest as it was the first house ever built in the city. You can see that a good deal has been added to it since then, as the museum now contains several large galleries in addition to the lobby. Moving straight ahead, we're now in the Local History exhibit. Over here we have a display showing the founding of the city, and around the room you can see displays about various other historical events. After you've enjoyed the displays in here, you may follow me into the next room, where we'll find a photograph gallery

NOTES

NOTES

NOTES

NOTES

BARRON'S BOOKS AND CDs TO HELP YOU SUCCEED IN ESL EXAMS

Barron's ESL Guide to American Business English
Focused to fit the needs of ESL students. Paperback handbook describes a variety of business writings and sample correspondence. Review section covers the basics of English grammar.
ISBN 978-0-7641-0594-4, $18.99, *Can$22.99*

The Ins and Outs of Prepositions, 2nd Edition
Written for ESL students, this book examines more than 60 prepositions and presents guidelines for the many different, sometimes tricky ways they are used in English.
ISBN 978-0-7641-4728-9, $12.99, *Can$14.99*

American Accent Training with 6 Audio CDs, 3rd Edition
This combination book/audio CD package provides innovative instruction for students and business people with pronunciation exercises covering all vowel sounds, consonants, blends, and diphthongs. Also includes nationality guides for 10 languages: Chinese, Japanese, Indian, Spanish, French, German, Russian, Korean, Arabic, and the U.S. Southern accent.
ISBN 978-1-4380-7165-7, $39.99, *Can$45.99*

American Accent Training: Grammar with 2 Audio CDs
This book and audio compact disc program instructs beginning, intermediate, and advanced students of English as a second language in the elements of grammar, presenting a grammar review that emphasizes speech and correct pronunciation. The compact discs combine grammar, vocabulary, pronunciation, reading, writing, comprehension, and the American accent into a simple, step-by-step learning process.
ISBN 978-0-7641-9651-5, $24.99, *Can$29.99*

Mastering The American Accent
This combination book and audio instructional program is designed to diminish the accents of men and women who speak English as their second language. Specific exercises concentrate on vowel sounds, problematic consonants such as V, W, B, TH, and the American R, employ correct syllable stress, link words for smoother speech flow, use common word contractions such as won't instead of will not, and more. Additional topics that often confuse ESL students are also discussed and explained. Enclosed with the book are four compact discs that use male and female voices to coach correct American-style pronunciation.
ISBN 978-0-7641-9582-2, $29.99, *Can$35.99*

Barron's Educational Series, Inc.
250 Wireless Blvd.
Hauppauge, NY 11788
Order toll-free: 1-800-645-3476

In Canada:
Georgetown Book Warehouse
34 Armstrong Ave.
Georgetown, Ont. L7G 4R9
Canadian orders: 1-800-247-7160

Prices subject to change without notice.

Available at your local book store
or visit **www.barronseduc.com**

(#6a) R11/13

Audio Track Titles

Key Word Strategies

	Track 1	Introduction
	Track 2	Complete Notes
	Track 3	Multiple-Choice Questions
Practice 2	Track 4	Passages 1 through 5

Listening Module

General Strategies

Practice 1	Track 5	Audio 1
	Track 6	Audio 2
	Track 7	Audio 3
	Track 8	Audio 4
Practice 2	Track 9	

Section 1—Conversation

Practice 1	Track 10	Conversations 1 through 5
Practice 2	Track 11	Conversations 1 through 5
Practice 3	Track 12	Conversations 1 through 5

Section 2—Talk

Practice 1	Track 13	Talks 1 through 5
Practice 2	Track 14	Talks 1 through 5
Practice 3	Track 15	Talks 1 through 5

Section 3—Discussion

Practice 1	Track 16	Conversations 1 through 5
Practice 2	Track 17	Conversations 1 through 4
Practice 3	Track 18	Conversations 1 through 5

Section 4—Talk or Lecture

Practice 1	Track 19	Talks 1 through 3
Practice 2	Track 20	Talks 1 through 3
Practice 3	Track 21	Talks 1 through 3

Strategy Review

	Track 22	Section 1
	Track 23	Section 2
	Track 24	Section 3
	Track 25	Section 4

Speaking Module

Part 1	Track 26	Practice 1
	Track 27	Practice 2

STAR WARS

DARTH MAUL

SON OF DATHOMIR

STAR WARS™

DARTH MAUL

SON OF DATHOMIR

Writer JEREMY BARLOW
Pencils JUAN FRIGERI
Inks MAURO VARGAS
Colors WES DZIOBA
Letterer MICHAEL HEISLER
Cover Art CHRIS SCALF

"HATE LEADS TO LOLLIPOPS"
Writer & Artist DAVE McCAIG

"BABY DARTH MAUL GOES TO THE DENTIST"
& "BABY DARTH MAUL"
Artist LUCAS MARANGON
Colors JASON HVAM
Letterer STEVE DUTRO

Assistant Editors FREDDYE LINS WITH PHILIP SIMON
Editors RANDY STRADLEY WITH DAVE LAND

Editor in Chief AXEL ALONSO
Chief Creative Officer JOE QUESADA
President DAN BUCKLEY

For Lucasfilm:
Senior Editor FRANK PARISI
Creative Director MICHAEL SIGLAIN
Lucasfilm Story Group PABLO HIDALGO, JAMES WAUGH, LELAND CHEE, MATT MARTIN

Collection Editor MARK D. BEAZLEY
Assistant Editor CAITLIN O'CONNELL
Associate Managing Editor KATERI WOODY
Senior Editor, Special Projects JENNIFER GRÜNWALD
VP Production & Special Projects JEFF YOUNGQUIST
SVP Print, Sales & Marketing DAVID GABRIEL
Book Designer ADAM DEL RE

SPECIAL THANKS TO FRANK PARISI & LUCASFILM, DEIDRE HANSEN, RODRIGO RAMOS DE PABLO, JEPH YORK, DOUG SHARK OF MYCOMICSHOP.COM, DON ALSAFI OF WWW.G-MART.COM, AND JEREMY SHORR OF TITANCOMICS.COM.

STAR WARS: DARTH MAUL — SON OF DATHOMIR. Contains material originally published in magazine form as STAR WARS: DARTH MAUL — SON OF DATHOMIR #1-4 and STAR WARS TALES #7-9. Second edition. First printing 2017. ISBN# 978-1-302-90846-1. Published by MARVEL WORLDWIDE, INC., a subsidiary of MARVEL ENTERTAINMENT, LLC. OFFICE OF PUBLICATION: 135 West 50th Street, New York, NY 10020. Printed in the U.S.A. DAN BUCKLEY, President, Marvel Entertainment; JOE QUESADA, Chief Creative Officer; TOM BREVOORT, SVP of Publishing; DAVID BOGART, SVP of Business Affairs & Operations, Publishing & Partnership; C.B. CEBULSKI, VP of Brand Management & Development, Asia; DAVID GABRIEL, SVP of Sales & Marketing, Publishing; JEFF YOUNGQUIST, VP of Production & Special Projects; DAN CARR, Executive Director of Publishing Technology; ALEX MORALES, Director of Publishing Operations; SUSAN CRESPI, Production Manager; STAN LEE, Chairman Emeritus. For information regarding advertising in Marvel Comics or on Marvel.com, please contact Vit DeBellis, Integrated Sales Manager, at vdebellis@marvel.com. For Marvel subscription inquiries, please call 888-511-5480. Manufactured between 9/15/2017 and 10/16/2017 by QUAD/GRAPHICS WASECA, WASECA, MN, USA.

10 9 8 7 6 5 4 3 2 1

SON OF DATHOMIR

After surviving his confrontation with Obi-Wan Kenobi on Naboo, and being saved from madness by the Dathomir witch Mother Talzin, Darth Maul has constructed a vast criminal syndicate known as the Shadow Collective, gathering the galaxy's most feared crime lords. Black Sun, the Pykes, and even the mighty Hutts have all fallen in line behind the dark warrior.

From a base of operations on the planet of Mandalore, Maul plots revenge against his many enemies. But Maul's lust for power and conquest has drawn a great enemy upon him — his former master, Darth Sidious.

Judging Maul a threat to his own designs, Sidious has defeated his former apprentice, ruthlessly murdering Maul's brother Savage Opress and leaving Maul beaten but, curiously, still alive and imprisoned....

1

STYGEON. HOME TO A SECRET PRISON KNOWN ONLY TO A FEW...
IT WOULD BE WISE TO KILL ME.
DO NOT MISTAKE THE FACT THAT I HAVE ALLOWED YOU TO LIVE FOR COMPASSION, MY FORMER APPRENTICE.

THERE IS A PURPOSE FOR EVERYTHING IN THE GALAXY...
...AND A WAY TO DESTROY IT.
I SEE YOU REMEMBER YOUR LESSONS.
YOU SUMMONED ME, MASTER?
AH, YES. MY APPRENTICE.
COME, COUNT DOOKU -- LET US LEAVE HERE. WE HAVE MUCH TO DISCUSS.
DOOKU...

THERE ARE MANY FORCES POISED AGAINST US. TO ENSURE OUR COMPLETE AND TOTAL VICTORY, WE MUST ROOT OUT AND DESTROY ALL OF OUR ENEMIES.
YOU SPEAK OF ENEMIES OTHER THAN THE JEDI?

I SPEAK OF THAT DATHOMIR WITCH -- MOTHER TALZIN.
THE REPORTS FROM GENERAL GRIEVOUS SUGGEST THAT SHE WAS KILLED WHEN HE INVADED DATHOMIR.
THE FACT THAT MAUL LIVES IS PROOF ENOUGH THAT GRIEVOUS FAILED TO DESTROY HER.

"MY HISTORY WITH THE DATHOMIR WITCHES GOES BACK FURTHER THAN YOU KNOW.
"MAUL CAME TO ME AS A CHILD -- A NOT-SO-APPRECIATED GIFT FROM MOTHER TALZIN.
"HER SPITE FOR ME RUNS DEEP..."

...AND THE TIME HAS COME FOR ME TO DEAL WITH HER.
WHAT WOULD YOU ASK OF ME, MY LORD?
MAUL HAS USED THE UNDERWORLD TO FORM A BASE OF POWER. FIND OUT WHAT YOU CAN.

IN THE END, WE SHALL USE MAUL TO LEAD US TO TALZIN.
WHY NOT SIMPLY SEND OUR ARMIES TO DATHOMIR?

BECAUSE SUCH METHODS CANNOT DEFEAT A WITCH THAT POWERFUL. TALZIN MUST BE COAXED INTO THE LIGHT...

...BEFORE SHE IS PERMANENTLY SNUFFED OUT.

ON THE OTHER SIDE OF THE SECRET PRISON...
?
KZZT!
KRENCH!
KRAK!

COMMANDER SAXON. WHAT IS YOUR STATUS?
WE FOLLOWED THE SHIP CARRYING MAUL TO STYGEON. OUR SCANS SHOW HE'S BEING HELD SOMEWHERE ON LEVEL SEVEN.

PROCEED WITH YOUR EXTRACTION. ONCE YOU HAVE HIM, RENDEZVOUS WITH OUR REMAINING FORCES ON ZANBAR.

IT SHALL BE DONE.

THE HUTTS HAVE ABANDONED YOU, MAUL. BUT BLACK SUN AND THE PYKES REMAIN LOYAL.
I WANT YOUR RESOURCES AND YOUR SWAY OVER THE BLACK MARKET.
YOU ARE DOOKU -- THE JEDI BETRAYER? I HAVE HEARD MUCH OF YOU SINCE MY REBIRTH.
I EXPECTED... MORE.
I'LL ASK THIS ONLY ONCE.
GIVE ME THE NAMES OF YOUR UNDERWORLD LEADERS AND THE LOCATIONS OF YOUR SHADOW COLLECTIVE BASES.
NEVER.
NNNGGAARRRRGH!!!
KNOW THAT THERE IS NOTHING YOU POSSESS THAT I CANNOT TAKE AWAY.
I HOPE OUR NEXT CONVERSATION WILL BE MORE FRUITFUL.

CHARGES PLACED AND PRIMED.
LIGHT THEM UP, KAST.

BOOM!
STATUS REPORT!
SOME KIND OF EXPLOSION ON LEVEL THREE, SIR!
ALERTING SECURITY AND DISPATCHING A FIRE CREW NOW!

LEVEL THREE?
SEND A GROUP OF DESTROYERS TO LEVEL SEVEN, AS WELL...

"...IF SOMEONE IS ATTEMPTING TO INFILTRATE THIS PRISON, I HAVE A FEELING THAT'S WHERE THEIR REAL TARGET LIES."

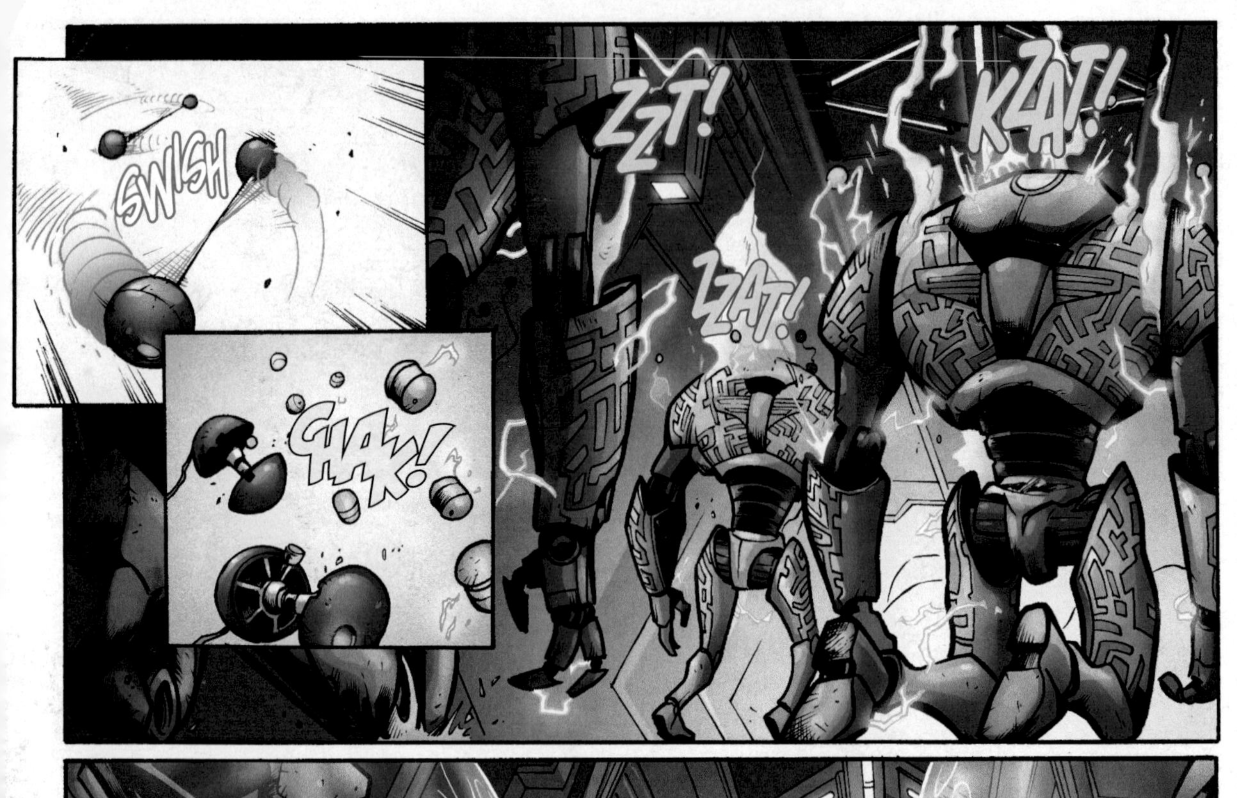
SWISH
CLAK!
ZZT!
KZAT!
ZZAT!

HIT THEM NOW!
FWOOSH!

KA-KROOOOM!!!

LORD MAUL -- WE'RE GOING TO GET YOU OUT OF HERE.
CAN YOU WALK?
MORE DROIDS COMING THIS WAY.
I HAVE BECOME INDIFFERENT TO PAIN.
THEY'RE STILL DOWN THE CORRIDOR.
THEN WE HAVE TIME.
THIS WAS YOUR PLAN?
YOU MIGHT WANT TO STEP BACK, LORD MAUL.
SHWOOM!

THOOM!
THIS WAS OUR PLAN.
DOW! BDOW!
SHUUK!

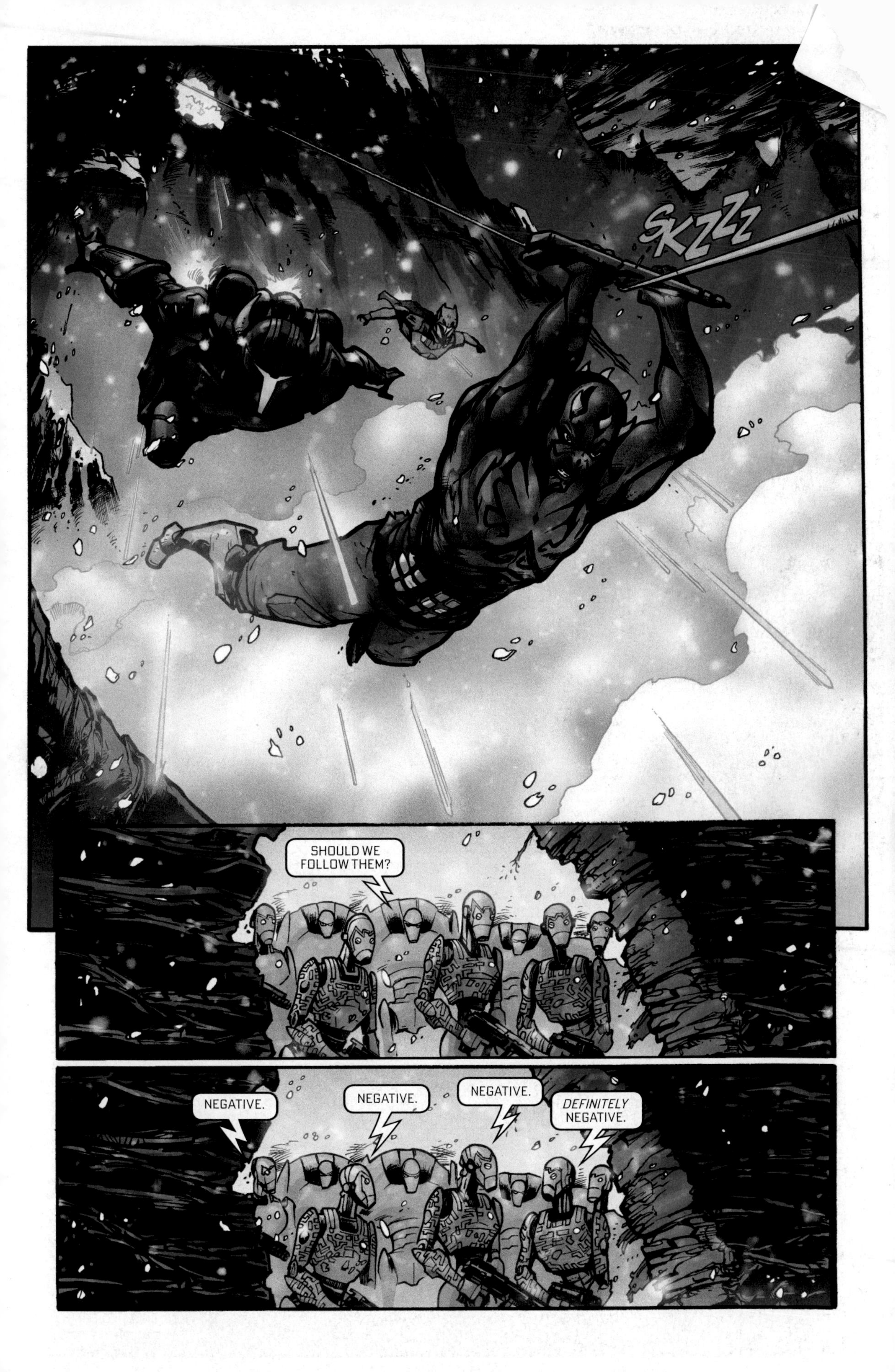
SKZZZ
SHOULD WE FOLLOW THEM?
NEGATIVE.
NEGATIVE.
NEGATIVE.
DEFINITELY NEGATIVE.

UH-OH.
DOW! DOW! DOW!
THOOM!
UM... BZZK
...IT LOOKS LIKE THE PRISONER HAS BZZK! ESCAPED, SIR.

SOON...
MAUL'S SHIP HAS BEEN TRACKED TO THE PLANET **ZANBAR**...
...DIRECT YOUR FLEET THERE AND ENGAGE HIM. HE'S HAD TIME TO MARSHAL HIS FORCES, SO BE PREPARED.
YOU SHOULD HAVE **KILLED** MAUL WHEN YOU HAD HIM IN YOUR CUSTODY. I TOLD YOU HE WAS **TOO DANGEROUS** TO LET LIVE.
DO NOT QUESTION THE PLANS OF MY MASTER.
REMEMBER -- YOU MUST **HURT** MAUL, BUT NOT DESTROY HIM. WEAKEN HIS FORCES, INJURE HIS PRIDE.

WHAT THEN, MY LORD?
THEN HE WILL DO WHAT ANY CHILD WOULD...

"...HE WILL CRY FOR HELP."
A SECRET SHADOW COLLECTIVE BASE ON THE SWAMP MOON ZANBAR.

PRIME MINISTER ALMEC. I HAVE YOU TO THANK FOR SECURING MY RELEASE?
YOU RELEASED ME FROM PRISON. I HAVE NOW RETURNED THE FAVOR.
WE RECOVERED THE DARK SABER FROM THE PALACE GROUNDS AFTER YOUR CAPTURE ON MANDALORE.

BLACK SUN AND THE PYKES STILL FOLLOW YOU, LORD MAUL -- AS DO WE. WHAT IS YOUR COMMAND?
THE WAR YOU HAVE WAITED YOUR ENTIRE LIVES TO FIGHT IS UPON US, MY BROTHERS!
VICTORY OR DEATH!

VICTORY OR DEATH!
VICTORY OR DEATH!
VICTORY OR DEATH!

INCOMING SEPARATIST DROP SHIPS! WE'RE UNDER ATTACK!
UNLEASH THE MIGHT OF THE SHADOW COLLECTIVE UPON THEM!
BDOW!
BDOW!
BDOW!
BDOW!
SHOOM!
THOOM!
THE MANDALORIANS' HEAVY FIREPOWER WON'T BE ENOUGH TO REPEL OUR DROP SHIPS.
GOOD. PRESS THE ATTACK...

"...DEPLOY OUR INFANTRY -- EVERY LAST SOLDIER.
"WE ARE NOT FIGHTING CLONES THIS TIME. THESE ARE MANDALORIAN WARRIORS.
"SEND IN EVERYTHING WE HAVE AND LET US HOPE THAT WILL BE ENOUGH.
"BECAUSE I CAN CALCULATE WITH CERTAINTY, BASED ON EXPERIENCE...
"...THE ODDS ARE STACKED AGAINST US!"

MAUL! YOUR END IS AT HAND!
GO SOFTEN HIM UP A BIT.
VMM
VVVM
THUCK

YOU COWARDS!

VMM
VMM
ZZT
VVZT
VRRT
ZWZZZT
SHUK
ARRGH!

TOO AFRAID TO MEET ME FACE TO FACE?
ZDOW!
DOW!
ZDOW!
ZDOW!
WE CAN DO IT THIS WAY, IF THAT'S WHAT YOU DESIRE.
VMM!
VMMM!
GRIEVOUS!

I'M MORE THAN A MATCH FOR YOU!
YOUR EFFORTS ARE USELESS! YOUR ARMY IS SKILLED, BUT MY FORCES ARE UNENDING!
LOOK AROUND -- YOUR MANDALORIANS HAVE BEEN CRUSHED!
"ONLY MY DROIDS REMAIN NOW --
"-- YOUR BATTLE IS ALREADY LOST!"
AAARRAAGGHH!!!

WE'RE NOT FINISHED YET.
MY GAUNTLET FIGHTERS HAVE YET TO ENTER THE FIGHT!
BOOM!
THOOM!

DROP DOWN TO LORD MAUL'S POSITION!
HA!
LORD MAUL -- I WAS AFRAID WE'D LOST YOU.
TAKE US AWAY FROM HERE, KAST...
...I CAN NO LONGER STOMACH THE SIGHT OF IT.

I HAVE DONE AS YOU ASKED -- I HAVE MADE MAUL **BLEED.**
HE AND HIS ARMY ARE NOW ON THE RUN.
WHAT WERE HIS LOSSES?

EXTENSIVE.
BUT IN TRUTH, I HAD ALL BUT EXHAUSTED MY OWN FORCES, AS WELL.

ACCEPTABLE LOSSES, GENERAL. YOU HAVE DONE WELL.
MAUL WILL BELIEVE THAT WE ARE ATTEMPTING TO DESTROY HIS POWER BASE AND DISRUPT HIS SYNDICATE.
HE MUST NOT LEARN OUR **TRUE** INTENTIONS.

THE WITCH, TALZIN?
YES. MY MASTER FEELS THESE ATTACKS WILL DRAW HER OUT INTO THE OPEN.
WHY WOULD SHE RISK HERSELF SO? WHAT VALUE DOES MAUL HOLD FOR HER?

ALL IN GOOD TIME, GENERAL.
YOU WILL SEE, ALL IN GOOD TIME.

"MOTHER...
"...MOTHER, I IMPLORE YOU..."
...I SEEK YOUR GUIDANCE.
DO NOT FIGHT ME, MY CHILD. BECOME MY VESSEL.
SPEAK TO ME, MY BELOVED SON.
I HAVE DONE AS YOU WISHED. THE POWER I AMASSED LURED YOUR ENEMY, **SIDIOUS.**
HE CAPTURED ME, BUT I ESCAPED HIS GRASP.
WE MUST ASSUME THAT HE **ALLOWED** YOU TO BREAK FREE.
WITH SIDIOUS, NOTHING IS EVER AS IT SEEMS. WE MUST BE THIS WAY, AS WELL.
YOU ARE WISE AS EVER, MOTHER.
GRIEVOUS AND HIS DROID ARMY HAVE DRIVEN US FROM ZANBAR. WE ARE WOUNDED BUT ALIVE.
WHAT IS YOUR GUIDANCE?

SIDIOUS WILL EXPECT YOU TO RETREAT TO MY PROTECTION. WE WILL NOT DO THIS.
LEAD YOUR FLEET TO ORD MANTELL. YOUR ALLIES -- BLACK SUN -- HAVE A STRONGHOLD THERE.
GATHER YOUR STRENGTH AND PREPARE YOURSELF. OUR NEXT MOVE IS CRITICAL.
WILL YOU MEET ME THERE, MOTHER?
I WILL NOT...
"...HOWEVER, AID FROM DATHOMIR SHALL SOON BE YOURS. OUR VICTORY WILL BE TOTAL AND COMPLETE."
ORD MANTELL.

"A BATTLE IS COMING, MY BROTHERS..."
...A BATTLE BETWEEN THE SITH AND THAT WHICH THEY FEAR THE MOST -- US.
YOU INSPIRE US ALL, LORD MAUL.
BUT DO YOU TRULY INTEND TO FIGHT COUNT DOOKU AND HIS SEPARATIST LEGIONS?
THEIR FORCES ARE MINDLESS DROIDS, ZITON MOJ. TAKE OUT THEIR LEADERSHIP AND THEY ALL FALL DOWN.
THESE CLONE WARS HAVE VASTLY OVEREXTENDED DOOKU AND GENERAL GRIEVOUS. THEY ARE MORE VULNERABLE THAN THEY REALIZE.
AND THEY REMAIN UNAWARE OF OUR TRUE NUMBERS.
PRECISELY, FIFE. WE CAN ATTACK THEM DIRECTLY.
WHEN DOOKU AND GRIEVOUS ARRIVE, WE'LL BE WAITING TO TRAP THEM IN THEIR OWN NET.

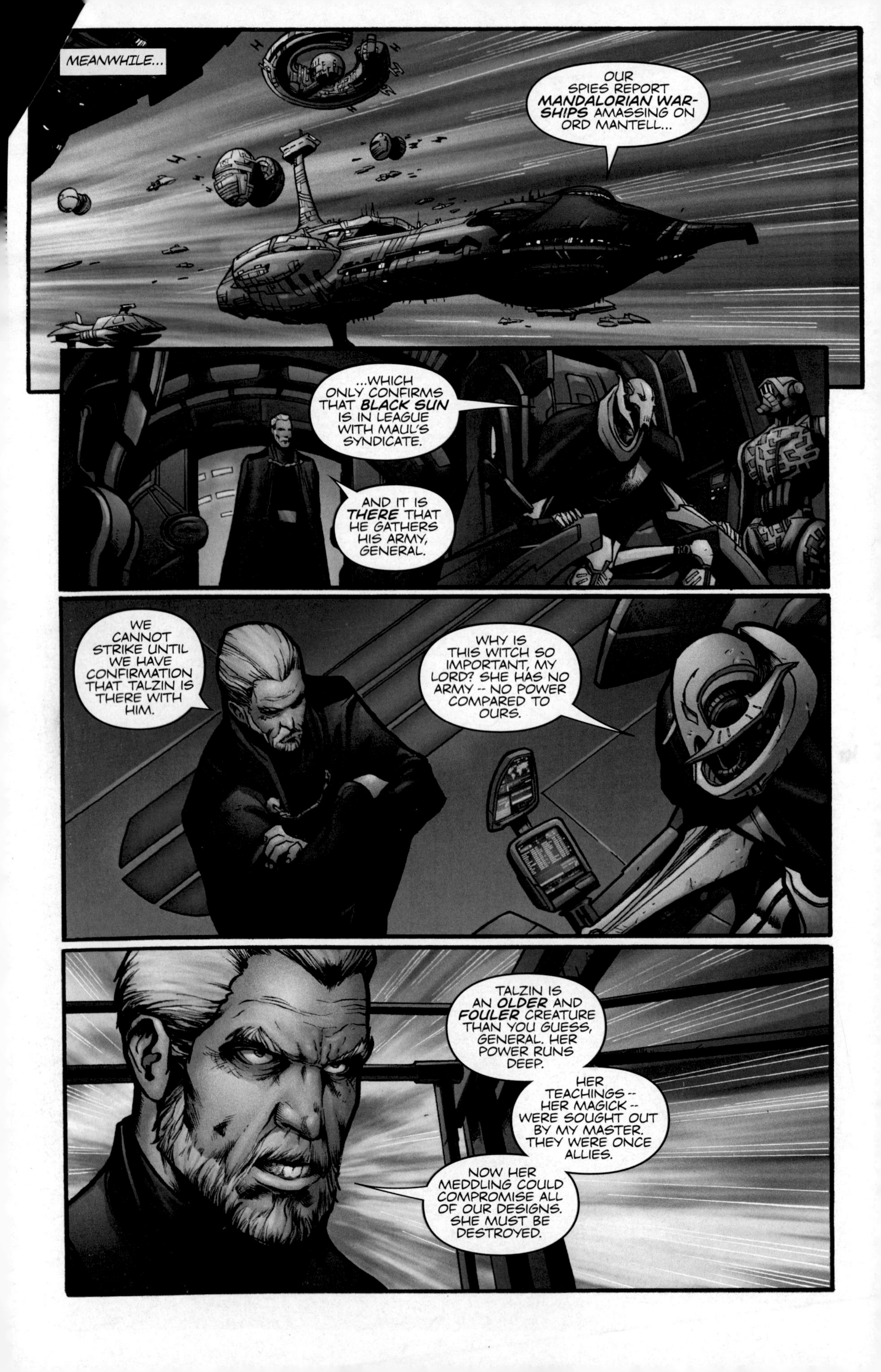
MEANWHILE...
OUR SPIES REPORT MANDALORIAN WAR-SHIPS AMASSING ON ORD MANTELL...
...WHICH ONLY CONFIRMS THAT BLACK SUN IS IN LEAGUE WITH MAUL'S SYNDICATE.
AND IT IS THERE THAT HE GATHERS HIS ARMY, GENERAL.
WE CANNOT STRIKE UNTIL WE HAVE CONFIRMATION THAT TALZIN IS THERE WITH HIM.
WHY IS THIS WITCH SO IMPORTANT, MY LORD? SHE HAS NO ARMY -- NO POWER COMPARED TO OURS.
TALZIN IS AN OLDER AND FOULER CREATURE THAN YOU GUESS, GENERAL. HER POWER RUNS DEEP.
HER TEACHINGS -- HER MAGICK -- WERE SOUGHT OUT BY MY MASTER. THEY WERE ONCE ALLIES.
NOW HER MEDDLING COULD COMPROMISE ALL OF OUR DESIGNS. SHE MUST BE DESTROYED.

SIR--RECONNAISSANCE DROIDS NEAR DATHOMIR REPORT A *SINGLE TRANS-PORT SHUTTLE* LEFT THE PLANET MOMENTS AGO.
WERE THEY ABLE TO SCAN THE SHIP?
UNABLE TO CONFIRM.
ALSO UNABLE TO DETERMINE ITS EXACT TRAJECTORY, BUT ORD MANTELL IS A POSSIBILITY.
THE WITCH MAY BE ATTEMPTING TO REACH MAUL EVEN AS WE SPEAK.
INPUT COORDINATES TO ORD MANTELL AND INSTRUCT THE FLEET TO FOLLOW US INTO HYPERSPACE.
WHEN WE ARRIVE, ***YOU*** WILL COMMAND THE BOMBARDMENT FROM ORBIT, GENERAL...
...AND YOU WILL LEAVE TALZIN TO ME.

SOON...
THEIR ATTACK WILL BEGIN BY AIR. GROUND FORCES WILL BE COMMITTED ONLY AFTER THEY BELIEVE THE BATTLE IS WON.
WE LURE THEM INTO THE CHOKEPOINTS HERE. USE THEIR NUMBERS AGAINST THEM...
"...ONCE WE DRAW THEM IN, THE MANDALORIANS WILL LEAD THE PYKES AND BLACK SUN'S MERCENARIES IN A FULL SCALE COUNTERATTACK.
"WHAT WE LACK IN NUMBERS, WE'LL MAKE UP IN SUPERIOR ABILITY AND MASTERY OF THE TERRAIN."
LORD MAUL -- WE HAVE AN INCOMING TRANSPORT FROM DATHOMIR.
SAXON -- WITH ME.
KAST -- BRING THE OTHERS UP TO SPEED ON THE REST OF MY PLAN.

LORD MAUL...
...I AM BROTHER VISCUS.
MOTHER TALZIN SENT US TO AID YOU.
NIGHT-BROTHERS. PURE WARRIORS.
MOTHER HAS CHOSEN WELL.
I SENSE...
THE DROIDS ARE HERE.

FIRE!
BDOW!
BDOW!
BDEW!
VA-VVMMMM!

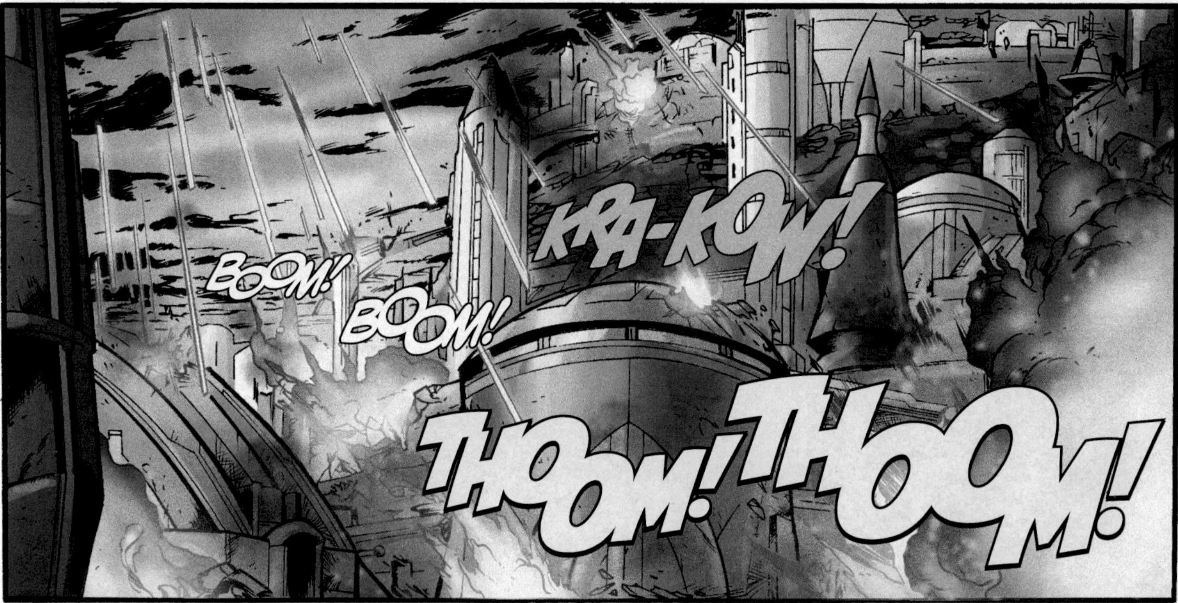
BOOM!
BOOM!
KRA-KOW!
THOOM! THOOM!

BDOW!
DOW! DOW! DOW!
KVOW!
BDEW!
BDEW!

BOOM!
THOOM!
THEY ARE UPON US! TAKE YOUR POSITIONS!

BROTHER VISCUS -- THERE IS NO TIME FOR A BRIEFING.
TAKE YOUR NIGHTBROTHERS TO MY COMMAND CENTER AND WAIT FOR MY WORD.

SAXON -- YOU KNOW WHAT TO DO.
PREPARE FOR THEIR GROUND ASSAULT. HOLD THEM AT BAY UNTIL WE'RE IN POSITION.

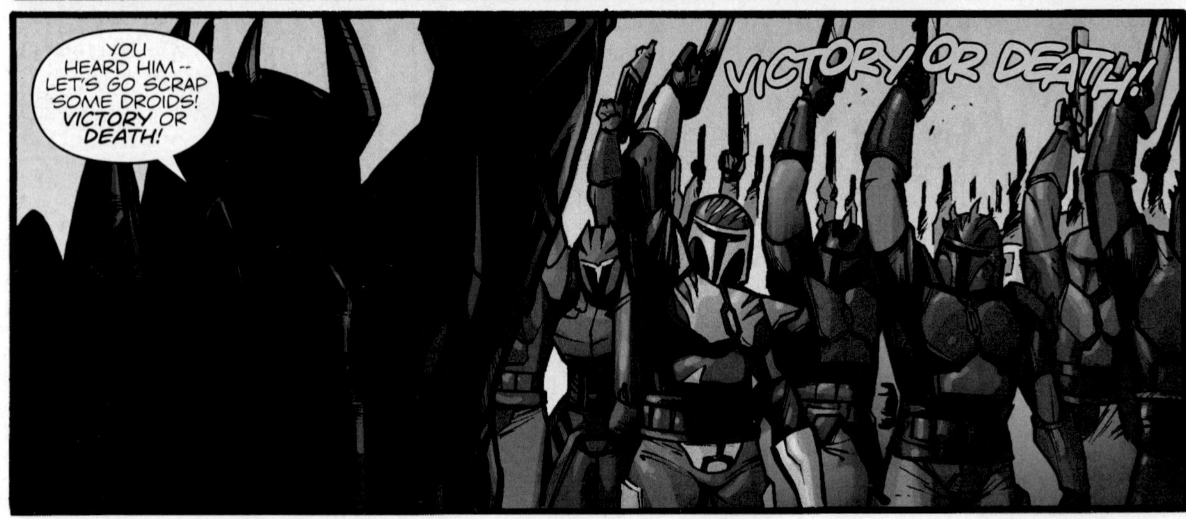
YOU HEARD HIM -- LET'S GO SCRAP SOME DROIDS! VICTORY OR DEATH!
VICTORY OR DEATH!

INFANTRY DEPLOYED, SIR.
GOOD, TEY-ZUKA. WE HAVE THEM ON THE RUN!
"ONCE OUR DROIDS TAKE CONTROL OF THE CITY --
"-- MAUL'S FORCES WILL BE *INSECTS* UNDER OUR *HEELS!*"

AT THAT SAME MOMENT...
KSSSH
FIND MAUL AND THE WITCH TALZIN -- NO OTHER TARGETS MATTER.
LEVEL THE CITY UNTIL THEY ARE FOUND!

ALL GUNNERY DECKS ARE RELOADED AND RECHARGED, SIR.
THE FLEET IS READY TO RESUME BOMDARDMENT ON YOUR ORDER.
NOT YET --
-- SOMETHING ISN'T RIGHT.
WE KNOW MAUL HAS SEVERAL MANDALORIAN WARSHIPS AT HIS DISPOSAL, BUT WE'VE SEEN NO AERIAL SUPPORT PROTECTING THE CITY...
...SO WHERE ARE THEY?
I CALCULATE THESE WARSHIPS WERE DESTROYED BEFORE THEY COULD LIFT OFF.
THOOM!
NO! THEY WEREN'T DESTROYED --

FOCUS ON THE COMMAND SHIP WHILE THE FLEET'S CANNONS ARE STILL AIMED AT THE PLANET...

...WHEN WE CAPTURE GRIEVOUS, THE DROID ARMIES WILL FALL ALONG WITH HIM.

MAUL WAS HERE --
GZZT!
ZZAT!
WELCOME, COUNT. MOTHER TALZIN SENDS HER REGARDS.
WE HAVE COME TO DEAL WITH YOU IN HER PLACE.
YOU WILL FIND THAT TASK BEYOND YOUR ABILITIES, NIGHT-BROTHERS.

THIS ISN'T A COUNTER-ATTACK -- IT'S A SLAUGHTER.
HE'S RIGHT!
I DON'T KNOW WHAT LORD MAUL'S BIG PLAN IS, BUT IT'S NOT WORKING.
REIN IT IN, SOLDIER. WE DON'T QUESTION THE STRATEGY -- WE ENSURE ITS SUCCESS.
WE JUST HAVE TO LAST LONG ENOUGH TO --
GAH!
KRAH!
AH! HELP ME!
BEYOO!
BEYOO!

CLOSER! BRING US IN CLOSER TO THE COMMAND SHIP!
THERE! AS SOON AS WE'RE UNDERNEATH THEIR FIRING RANGE -- ATTACH TO THEIR SHIP!
"PREPARE A BOARDING PARTY...
SSZZT!
ZZZSSSSH
"...WE'RE GOING TO TAKE THIS FIGHT RIGHT TO GRIEVOUS!"

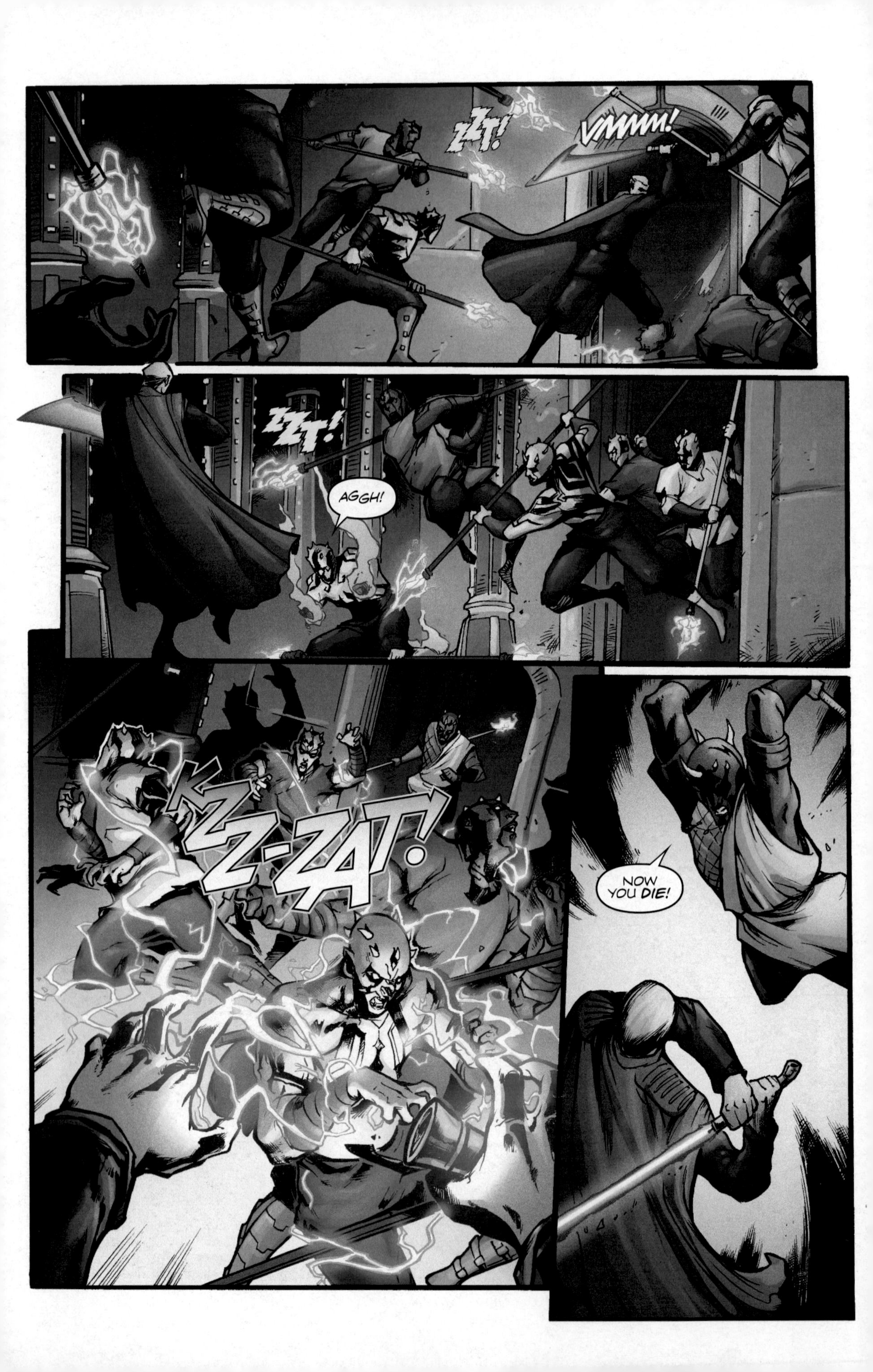
ZZZT!
VMMM!
ZZZT!
AGGH!
KZZ-ZAT!
NOW YOU DIE!

THEY HAVE BOARDED OUR SHIP!
I AM UNABLE TO--
ONE WARNING -- DISCONNECT THE DROIDS' COMMAND SIGNAL...
KWAM! SMASH!
...OR DIE.
UH-OH.
GURRF!
OR DO BOTH -- IT MATTERS NOT TO ME.

WHAT DO WE DO WITH THEM?
OUR ORDERS ARE TO TAKE NO PRISONERS.
YOU FOUGHT HARD, MEN. IT'S BEEN AN HONOR.
VRRRRMMM
THEIR COMMAND SIGNAL JUST WENT DEAD!
TEAR THEM APART!

YOU ARE FORMIDABLE, COUNT -- THIS WILL BE A VICTORY WELL EARNED.
KNOW THIS, BROTHER VISCUS --
!
-- I WILL DESTROY YOU...THEN MAUL --
-- AND FINALLY TALZIN.
KRUMF!
YOUR PEOPLE WILL BE BUT A MEMORY.
THAT'S FAR ENOUGH, DOOKU!

LATER...
IT IS DONE, MOTHER.
DOOKU AND GRIEVOUS HAVE BEEN CAPTURED. WE NOW CONTROL THEIR FORCES.
YOU HAVE DONE WELL, MY SON.
SOON SIDIOUS WILL FOLLOW...
...AND TOGETHER WE WILL HAVE OUR REVENGE.

3

DARTH MAUL?
SO IT WOULD SEEM, MASTER JEDI.
THE CITIZENS WHO SURVIVED THE BLITZ ON ORD MANTELL IDENTIFIED COUNT DOOKU LEADING THE CHARGE AGAINST A RED-SKINNED FORCE WIELDER OF SOME TYPE.
COULD THIS BE THE "ROGUE SITH" YOU'VE BEEN SEARCHING FOR?
IF HE IS, AND IF HE AND DOOKU ARE FIGHTING AGAINST EACH OTHER...
...PERHAPS THE REPUBLIC CAN USE THIS INTEL TO CAPTURE THEM BOTH AND FINALLY END THIS WAR.
BY ALL MEANS -- DO WHATEVER IT TAKES. WHATEVER RESOURCES YOU REQUIRE --

"-- BRING THESE VILLAINS TO JUSTICE BEFORE THEY INFLICT ANY MORE HARM ON THE GALAXY."
ORD MANTELL CITY.
THIS JUST GOT MORE INTERESTING.
BLIP!
WHAT DO WE KNOW, MASTER KENOBI?
IT'S CLEAR THE SEPARATIST DROID ARMY BATTLED AGAINST A MASSIVE FORCE HERE, BUT EXACTLY WHAT THAT FORCE WAS REMAINS ELUSIVE.
IT'S AS IF THE OPPOSING SOLDIERS TOOK CARE TO COLLECT ALL TRACE OF THEIR PRESENCE ON THEIR WAY OUT.
NOT ALL, TIPLEE.
COMMANDER WOLFFE AND HIS MEN UNCOVERED THIS JUST OUTSIDE THE CITY WALLS.
MANDALORIANS?
THIS CONFIRMS OUR INTEL FROM THE MANDALORE RESISTANCE THAT THE ALLIANCE BETWEEN PRIME MINISTER ALMEC AND THE UNDERWORLD IS STILL INTACT.

WE KNOW THAT BLACK SUN HAS A FOOTHOLD HERE. COULD THE SHADOW COLLECTIVE BE STAGING A MAJOR OPERATION IN THAT SECTOR?

DEET! DEET!
THERE IS A KNOWN MANDALORIAN SUPPLY OUTPOST IN THIS SYSTEM.

MAUL COULD BE LURKING IN THE SHADOWS THERE.

WE CAN'T LET MANDALORE FALL INTO THE HANDS OF THE SEPARATISTS.
I AGREE.
MASTER TIPLEE AND I WILL INVESTIGATE THAT OUTPOST --

"-- AND SEE WHAT COMES SCURRYING OUT WHEN WE SHINE A LIGHT ON IT."
LORD TYRANUS -- YOU DISAPPOINT ME.
NOW YOU SEE THEIR FAILURE -- AND YET YOU COULD NOT FORESEE THE TRAP I LAID FOR THEM.
YOUR SCHEMES ARE UNRAVELING, SIDIOUS. WITHOUT YOUR GENERALS, YOUR ARMIES WILL BE CRUSHED -- AS WILL YOUR "PLANS."
THAT ONLY PROVES THEIR WEAKNESS, NOT MY OWN. WHAT ARE YOUR DEMANDS?
NOT MY DEMANDS -- MOTHER TALZIN'S.

YES -- YOU REMEMBER THE MOTHER!
SHE WAS YOUR ALLY, BUT YOU USED HER AS YOU USED ME BEFORE THROWING US BOTH AWAY. AS YOU WILL THESE TWO.

KILL THEM. I HAVE NO MORE USE FOR EITHER ONE OF THEM.

SO BE IT. SINCE NEW APPRENTICES ARE APPARENTLY SO EASY TO FIND...

TREAD LIGHTLY, MAUL. REVENGE IS A DANGEROUS GAME...
...ONE YOU NEVER SEEM TO WIN.
I ONLY LOST WHEN I FOLLOWED YOU, OLD MAN.
BLIP!
WHAT DO WE DO WITH THESE TWO?
TAKE THAT MONSTROSITY TO THE BRIG AND PUT HIM UNDER CONSTANT WATCH.
LEAVE COUNT DOOKU AND ME ALONE. WE HAVE MUCH TO DISCUSS.
IT WOULD BE UNFORTUNATE IF NEXT TIME WE MET, COUNT, I HAD TO ADD YOUR LIGHTSABER TO MY COLLECTION.
WE ALL HAVE OUR PARTS TO PLAY, GENERAL...

"...I LOOK FORWARD TO OUR NEXT ENCOUNTER."
I SENSE YOUR TURMOIL, OBI-WAN.

MY LAST ENCOUNTER WITH MAUL DIDN'T GO SO WELL.
HE MURDERED THE DUCHESS SATINE. SOMEONE YOU CARED FOR DEEPLY.

MY EMOTIONS ARE UNDER CONTROL, MASTER TIPLEE.
I WILL NOT FAIL YOU OR THIS MISSION.

GENERAL KENOBI -- PROBES ARE LAUNCHED AND GUNSHIPS ARE READY TO SCRAMBLE ON YOUR ORDER...

"...IF MAUL IS HIDING IN THERE, WE'LL DRAG HIM OUT."
I LEFT YOU HERE TO MAKE YOU AN OFFER. WHILE GRIEVOUS IS A CREATURE OF LIMITED SCOPE, YOU SEE MUCH MORE.
YOU ABANDONED THE JEDI WHEN YOU UNDERSTOOD THE SITH WERE GAINING POWER.
NOW I SUGGEST YOU ABANDON SIDIOUS AND SERVE ME.
DO YOU REALLY BELIEVE THERE IS ANY POWER IN THE GALAXY THAT CAN STAND AGAINST MY LORD?
TEN THOUSAND JEDI KNIGHTS WILL TRY THIS AND ALL WILL FAIL. WHAT HOPE WILL YOUR ARMY HAVE?
WHAT HOPE WILL YOU HAVE?
MOTHER TALZIN HAS SHOWN ME THE REAL POWER -- I HAVE SEEN THE TRUTH.
SIDIOUS IS WEAKER THAN WE REALIZE. HE FEARS MOTHER, AND THAT --
-- WITH OUR COMBINED STRENGTH -- WILL BE HIS UNDOING.
OUR COMBINED STRENGTH?
WHEN MOTHER TALZIN AND I LAST MET SHE TRIED TO DESTROY ME.
THINGS HAVE CHANGED.

COUNT DOOKU.
FORGIVE OUR PREVIOUS DISAGREEMENTS. YOU WERE ONLY FOLLOWING YOUR MASTER'S WILL.
SIDIOUS IS DECEIVING YOU -- AS HE ONCE DECEIVED ME.
THEN YOU KNOW TO BETRAY THE DARK LORD IS FOLLY.

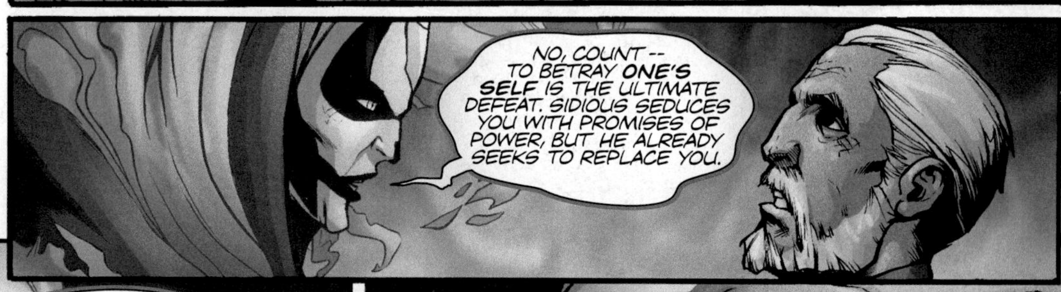
NO, COUNT -- TO BETRAY ONE'S SELF IS THE ULTIMATE DEFEAT. SIDIOUS SEDUCES YOU WITH PROMISES OF POWER, BUT HE ALREADY SEEKS TO REPLACE YOU.

LONG AGO, SIDIOUS CAME TO ME ON DATHOMIR. WE EXCHANGED SECRET WISDOM -- MINGLED DARK SIDE ABILITIES WITH NIGHTSISTER MAGICKS.
HE PROMISED TO MAKE ME HIS RIGHT HAND, BUT INSTEAD HE STOLE WHAT WAS MOST DEAR TO ME... MY OWN FLESH AND BLOOD.
MY SON!

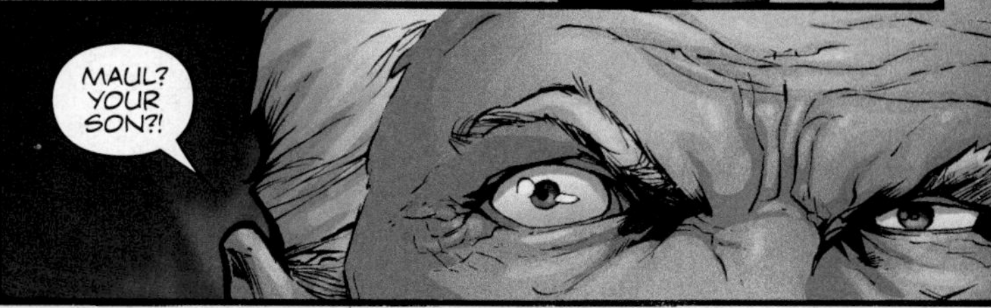
MAUL? YOUR SON?!

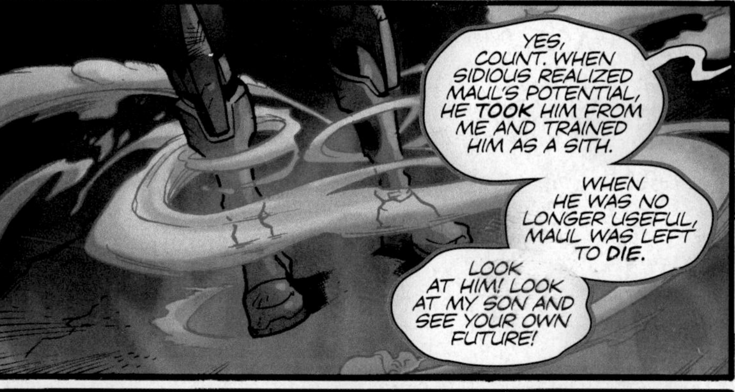
YES, COUNT. WHEN SIDIOUS REALIZED MAUL'S POTENTIAL, HE TOOK HIM FROM ME AND TRAINED HIM AS A SITH.
WHEN HE WAS NO LONGER USEFUL, MAUL WAS LEFT TO DIE.
LOOK AT HIM! LOOK AT MY SON AND SEE YOUR OWN FUTURE!

SIDIOUS WILL BETRAY YOU, AS HE BETRAYED US -- BUT I WILL HONOR OUR ALLIANCE SHOULD YOU ACCEPT IT.
JOIN US. TOGETHER WE CAN DESTROY SIDIOUS AND RULE THE GALAXY...OR YOU CAN CHOOSE TO DIE HERE ALONE.

A MILITARY BASE HIDDEN AMONG THE ASTEROIDS? ARE YOU CERTAIN?
NO DOUBT ABOUT IT. WE FINALLY HAVE THAT RED-FACED MONSTER IN OUR CROSS-HAIRS.
WITH MAUL, NOTHING IS AS IT APPEARS, CODY...
...LET'S MOVE WHILE WE STILL HAVE THE ELEMENT OF SURPRISE ON OUR SIDE.
MY LORD -- WE HAVE INCOMING REPUBLIC SHIPS!
BLOCK THEIR TRANSMISSIONS BEFORE THEY CAN SCAN US!
IT'S TOO LATE FOR THAT...
DEET!

"...THEY ALREADY KNOW THAT WE'RE HERE!"

DEET!

FSSSH
PERHAPS YOU ARE NOT SO USELESS AFTER ALL, COUNT!

MAUL'S STRONGHOLD IS IN SIGHT, GENERAL.
BRING US IN AS CLOSE AS YOU CAN WITHOUT DRAWING THEIR ATTENTION.

COPY THAT. WAIT UNTIL YOU SEE THIS PLACE -- IT'S NOT JUST HIDDEN **AMONG** THE ASTEROIDS...
...IT'S BUILT RIGHT INTO THE **SIDE** OF ONE!

THEY'RE LAUNCHING GAUNTLET FIGHTERS!

PUNCH THROUGH THOSE SHIPS AND GET US INTO THAT HANGAR!
HOLD ON!
KRASH!
SSSSSKKS!
I SENSE MAUL'S PRESENCE.
LET'S LOCK THIS PLACE DOWN UNTIL OUR REINFORCEMENTS ARRIVE.
WITH PLEASURE, MASTER KENOBI.

THOSE OF YOU WHO CAN STILL STAND -- RETURN TO YOUR MASTER...

...AND TELL HIM TO SEND MORE MEN!
KRUNCH!
AH. HOW CONVENIENT.
VOOM!

WE'VE BEEN BOARDED -- TWO JEDI HAVE BEEN SPOTTED IN HANGAR THREE!
WHAT'S IT GOING TO BE, COUNT?

ALLIES... OR DEATH?

LET US GO KILL SOME JEDI TOGETHER.

VVVVZZT!

WISE DECISION.

KEEP PRESSING FORWARD! WE HAVE TO REACH THE COMMAND CENTER --
OR BETTER YET -- LET US COME TO YOU.
SO IT *IS* TRUE -- YOU *ARE* WORKING TOGETHER!
OF COURSE. ONLY OUR SHARED HATRED OF *YOU* COULD BE STRONG ENOUGH TO UNITE US!

MORE GUNSHIPS!
STAND DOWN IN THE NAME OF THE REPUBLIC...
...THIS HAS GONE FAR ENOUGH, DOOKU!
AGREED. I CAN PROMISE YOU THAT YOUR DEATHS *WON'T* BE REMEMBERED.

FINALLY, A FAIR FIGHT!
ZZAAAZT!
ZZZT!
NNGH!
UHH!
KRAK!
THERE! PREPARE YOUR ROCKETS!
COME HERE, LITTLE JEDI...

ACK!
...I HAVE SOMETHING TO SHOW YOU.
MASTER TIPLEE!
AIM FOR THE TWI'LEK!
LORD MAUL --!
VOOOOSH!

-- INCOMING!
THOOM!
THIS WAY, LORD -- YOUR FIGHTER IS READY TO GO!
THEY'RE HEADING FOR THE GAUNTLETS!
DON'T LET THEM ESCAPE!

DON'T WORRY, KENOBI -- WE'LL BE SEEING EACH OTHER AGAIN SOON ENOUGH!

GET US OUT OF HERE.

SOON...
WHAT JUST HAPPENED?
GENERAL -- THE CHANCELLOR WOULD LIKE A WORD.

IT PAINS ME TO HEAR OF THIS TRAGEDY.
IT APPEARS THAT COUNT DOOKU AND DARTH MAUL ARE ALLIES NOW, WHICH COULD SOLVE A LONG-STANDING MYSTERY...

...WHICH IS THAT DOOKU IS THE SITH MASTER WE HAVE BEEN SEEKING ALL ALONG, AND MAUL IS THE APPRENTICE.

FASCINATING.
STILL, IS THERE NO EXPLANATION FOR THE BATTLE ON ORD MANTELL? HOW CAN THEY BE ENEMIES ONE MOMENT AND ALLIES THE NEXT?

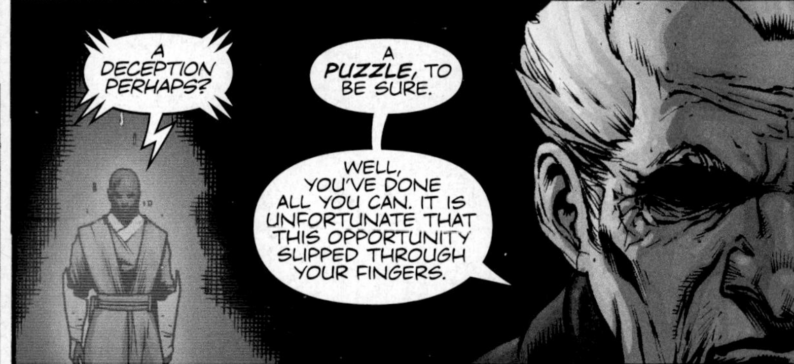
A DECEPTION PERHAPS?
A PUZZLE, TO BE SURE.
WELL, YOU'VE DONE ALL YOU CAN. IT IS UNFORTUNATE THAT THIS OPPORTUNITY SLIPPED THROUGH YOUR FINGERS.

I FEAR IN THE END IT COULD PROVE DISASTROUS FOR THE REPUBLIC.

4

BLACK SUN AND THE PYKES JOINED YOUR COLLECTIVE ON THE PROMISE OF GREATER PROFITS, **MAUL**. BUT THIS IS BECOMING YOUR OWN PERSONAL CRUSADE --

-- ONE THAT'S ALREADY COST US **ZANBAR**, **ORD MANTELL**, AND THE MANDALORIAN **ASTEROID OUTPOST**.
PERHAPS YOUR PLAN ISN'T AS SURE AS YOU SAY.

YOU'LL BE PAID -- IF THAT'S ALL YOU WANT.
IN THE MEANTIME, RETURN TO YOUR RESPECTIVE SECTORS AND PREPARE FOR OUR NEXT PHASE...

... ONCE DARTH SIDIOUS IS DEAD, THE GALAXY WILL BE ***OURS*** FOR THE TAKING.

KEEP THEM IN LINE.
YES, MY LORD.
YOU'RE LEARNING THAT SEIZING CONTROL --
-- IS MUCH EASIER THAN MAINTAINING IT.
WHAT WOULD YOU KNOW OF CONTROL, COUNT?
OUR "ALLIANCE" HAS BEEN SIDIOUS'S WILL ALL ALONG.
HE HAS INSTRUCTED YOU TO PLAY THIS GAME -- BUT YOU'VE BEEN OUTMATCHED.
I LOOK FORWARD TO WATCHING ALL OF THIS COME CRASHING DOWN AROUND YOU.

DATHOMIR.

BROTHER VISCUS -- I BRING YOU THE SPOILS OF WAR.
HAVE THE PREPARATIONS BEEN MADE?

WE ARE READY TO PROCEED.
YOU'LL FIND THIS TO BE QUITE A DIFFERENT EXPERIENCE THAN ORD MANTELL, COUNT.

COME, DOOKU -- WE ARE AT THE HEART OF MOTHER TALZIN'S POWER NOW...
...AND YOU ARE ABOUT TO ANSWER FOR YOUR MASTER'S CRIMES AGAINST THE NIGHTSISTERS.
GREAT MOTHER, HEAR OUR PRAYER.
DIVINER OF TRUTH. DELIVERER OF JUSTICE...
...REVEAL YOURSELF.
MY SON IS RIGHT, COUNT -- IT IS TIME TO ELIMINATE EVERYTHING THAT GIVES SIDIOUS POWER.
BEGINNING WITH YOU!
NNGAAGH!!!

MEANWHILE, IN ORBIT...
IT IS JUST AS YOU PREDICTED, MY LORD...
...WE'VE TRACED COUNT DOOKU'S SIGNAL TO DATHOMIR'S SURFACE.
WHAT IS YOUR COMMAND?
JAM THEIR COMMUNICATIONS AND CLOAK THIS SHIP FROM VIEW...
"...THEY WON'T KNOW WE'VE ARRIVED UNTIL IT'S MUCH TOO LATE."

YOU FEEL THAT, COUNT?
MOTHER DRAWS YOUR VERY LIFE FORCE FROM YOUR WITHERED BONES...

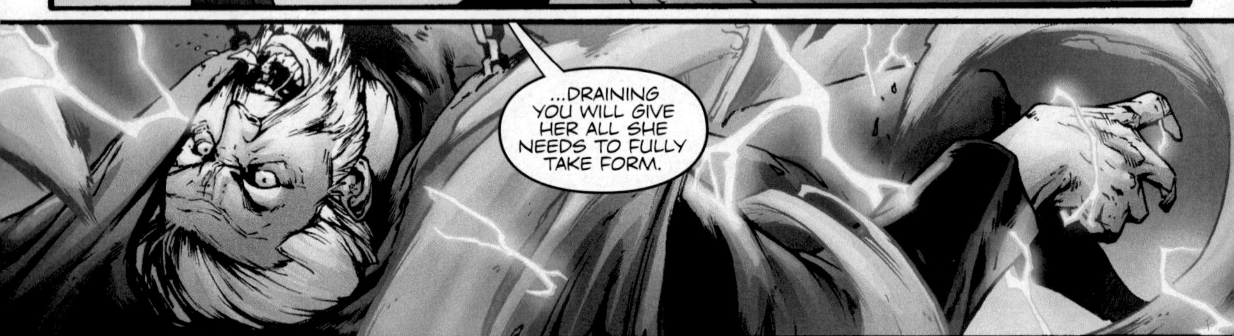
...DRAINING YOU WILL GIVE HER ALL SHE NEEDS TO FULLY TAKE FORM.

IT WON'T BE LONG NOW. HE WON'T SURVIVE THIS.
GOOD.

MOTHER WILL BE WHOLE SOON, BUT THE PROCESS COULD WEAKEN HER.
I'LL MAKE SURE HER CHAMBERS ARE READY.

AS A SITH, YOU UNDERSTAND DECEPTION. WITCHES DON'T DIE SO EASILY.
MOTHER SACRIFICED MUCH OF HER OWN FORM TO RESURRECT ME. THIS IS WHY YOU'VE BEEN UNABLE TO DETECT HER.
FOR HER, A COMPLETE AND PERMANENT RETURN TO THE PHYSICAL REALM REQUIRES GREAT SACRIFICE.
THROUGH YOUR BLOOD A NEW POWER WILL RISE FROM THE ROOTS OF DATHOMIR!
THOOM!

BLOOD IS ABOUT TO SPILL, ALL RIGHT.
YOURS!
YOU'RE TOO LATE, GENERAL. OUR PLANS ARE IN MOTION AND THEY CAN'T BE STOPPED.
NO MATTER HOW MANY TIMES YOU FAIL, YOU NEVER LEARN THIS LESSON, MAUL...
...THERE IS ONLY ONE PLAN -- ONE GREAT DESIGN WHICH SHALL GOVERN THE UNIVERSE --
-- MINE.

I'M TELLING YOU -- A FULL ARMADA OF DROID VESSELS JUST APPEARED OUT OF NOWHERE AND IS LAYING SIEGE TO OUR DEFENSES.
IT'S HAPPENING HERE, TOO -- THEY WERE LYING IN WAIT FOR US! HOW COULD THEY KNOW?!

WHERE IS MAUL? WE SHOULD BE DEALING DIRECTLY WITH HIM!

FOLLOW YOUR ORDERS. HUNKER DOWN AND **FIGHT.**
LORD MAUL'S LOCATION ISN'T YOUR CONCERN.

NOT OUR CONCERN?
IF HIS FLEET ISN'T DEPLOYED TO DEFEND US **IMMEDIATELY,** OUR PARTNERSHIP IS **FINISHED.**

NOW HOLD ON -- BLACK SUN HAS **MORE** THAN ENOUGH RESOURCES TO PROTECT ITSELF. **WE'RE** THE ONES WHO NEED SUPPORT!

AT LAST. THE GREAT DECEIVER COMES TO RESCUE HIS PAWN.
I COME TO END THIS FARCE ONCE AND FOR ALL.
YOU COME TO YOUR DOOM, OLD MAN.
MOTHER TALZIN LIVES --
-- AND YOUR APPRENTICE IS UNDER HER FULL CONTROL!
NOW, SIDIOUS -- YOU WILL PAY FOR YOUR BETRAYAL.

WVM
WVM
KZZT

SZZK

KSSAAH!
KKZT
VVVSH
YOU CONTROL DOOKU'S BODY, BUT YOU POSSESS NONE OF HIS SKILL.

RELEASE MY APPRENTICE, HAGGARD WITCH!

AAAAAAGH!!
AAAGH! AAAGHHH!!
ZZZAT
EEE-ENOUGH!

I AM WHOLE! I AM RETURNED!
YOU ARE ABOUT TO DIE.

FORGET THIS -- WE'VE LOST TOO MANY SHIPS! TELL MAUL HE'S ON HIS OWN!
THIS WHOLE ENDEAVOR HAS BECOME A **MASSIVE** LIABILITY. BLACK SUN IS FINISHED HERE, AS WELL.
THIS ISN'T WHAT WE AGREED!

YOU'RE THE WARRIOR. WE'RE MERCENARIES -- AND THERE'S NO MORE PROFIT IN THIS FIGHT.
IF YOU ABANDON YOUR POSTS I WILL HUNT YOU DOWN AND KILL YOU MYSELF!

ASSUMING YOU SURVIVE THE DAY.
SIR -- WE'RE PICKING UP SOMETHING **BIG** HEADING THIS WAY...
"...A ***SEPARATIST INVASION FLEET*** IS APPROACHING!"

UHN!
GOOD RIDDANCE, MECHANICAL TRASH.
HOW LONG I HAVE WAITED FOR THIS!
KZZZT
ZZZZAT
YES, YOUR RUSH TO OBLIVION HAS NEARLY REACHED ITS END.
KRZZAT

UGH...
THWIP
KZZZT
ZAKZZT
MOTHER! TAKE MY STRENGTH!

ZZZAK
KZZZT
FIGHT, MOTHER! FIGHT!

VOOSH
LORD MAUL! DATHOMIR IS LOST!
WE MUST RETREAT!
GO, MY SON.
WE CAN ESCAPE TOGETHER!
NOT THIS TIME. IF I LOWER MY DEFENSES, YOU WILL DIE.

OOF!
RUN!
MOTHER!
WE HAVE TO RUN, LORD MAUL! IF YOU DIE, EVERYTHING IS LOST!
LET GO OF ME!
KZZZZSH

IT'S TIME.
WM
VMMM
MOTHER -- NO!
HCK!

NO!
NO!

THAT WITCH NEVER LEARNED -- THERE ARE THOSE WITH POWER, AND THOSE WHO **DREAM** OF POWER...
...AND HER EXISTENCE WAS NOTHING BUT A DREAM.

MY LORD -- FORGIVE ME.
MAUL HAS ONCE AGAIN SLIPPED THROUGH MY GRASP.
NO, COUNT -- EVERYTHING HAPPENED AS FORESEEN.
THIS WAS A DIFFICULT PIECE TO MANEUVER, BUT NOW IT IS IN PLACE. MAUL'S FUTURE HAS BEEN ERASED...
"...WHILE **OURS** IS MORE CERTAIN THAN IT HAS EVER BEEN."
THE END

Lil' Maul in:
HATE LEADS TO LOLLIPOPS
HAPPY NERF HERDER
MAXIMUM SECURITY
HOME FOR WAYWARD BOYS
RIBhutt
KABOOM!
BREEEA! BREEEA!

BREEEA!
BREEEA!
SCREE!
FISH MARKET

YOINK!

SWOOOSH
MON CALAMARI FISH MARKET

!
DANGER
EXPLOSIVE
THUMP!

DANGER
TINK!

KAFWAAAM!

RIB hutt
Home of the "Rancor Ribs"
VVVVVVV

VVVVVVV

POW!

HOO!
WUDDA
WUDDA
SMASH!

CRASH!
WUDDA
WUDDA
BOOM!
WUDDA
WUDDA

TAKE

hop!
VMM

ZZZ

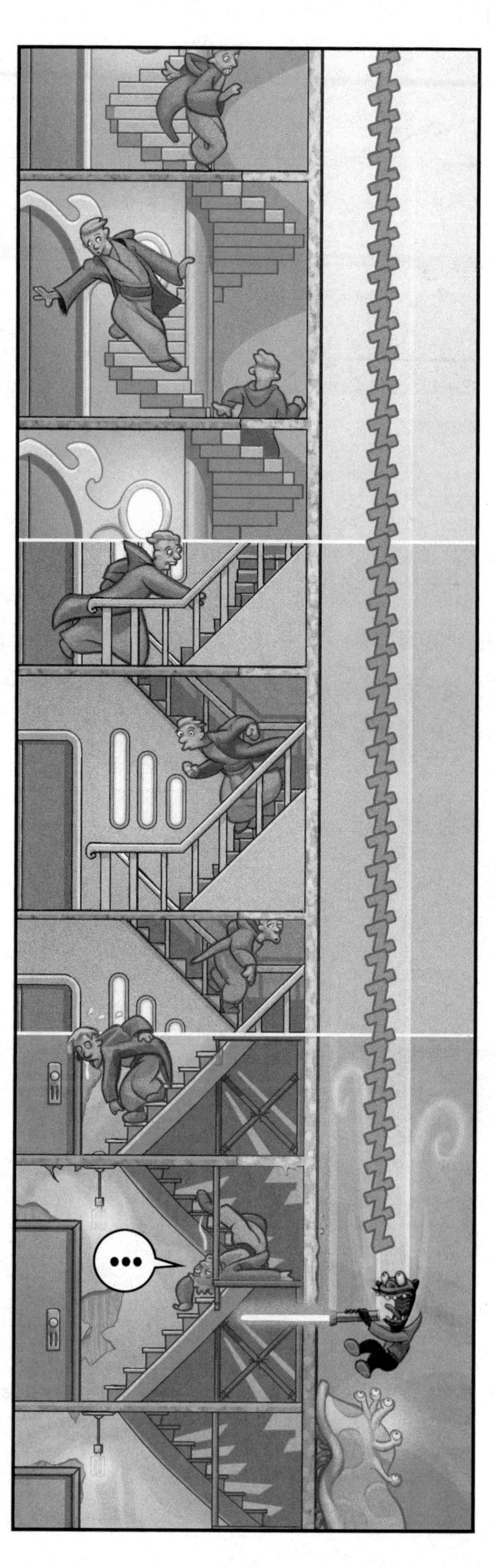
...

DOINK!

AAAAAA!

REEEOW

KER - FWAMM

Yank!

HOO, HOO! MY YOUNG *FRIEND*. YOU'VE PROVEN YOURSELF *QUITE* THE LITTLE TROUBLE MAKER!
...WELL, I HAVE YOU *NOW!*

UH... *SENATOR PALPATINE?* SHOULDN'T I BE DRAGGING HIM BACK TO THE *HOME FOR BOYS?*
NO,NO. HE *OBVIOUSLY* NEEDS BETTER GUIDANCE.
...I THINK I'LL TEND TO *HIS* RE-EDUCATION *PERSONALLY*.
Fin.

Art - Lucas Marangon
Colors - Jason Hvam
Letters - Steve Dutro

Art - Lucas Marangon
Colors - Jason Hvam
Letters - Steve Dutro

STAR WARS: DARTH MAUL — SON OF DATHOMIR 1
SAN DIEGO COMIC-CON VARIANT BY CHRIS SCALF

STAR WARS: DARTH MAUL — SON OF DATHOMIR 1

STAR WARS: DARTH MAUL — SON OF DATHOMIR 1
WIZARDWORLD SKETCH VARIANT BY CHRIS SCALF

STAR WARS: DARTH MAUL — SON OF DATHOMIR 1
DIAMOND RETAILER VARIANT BY CHRIS SCALF

STAR WARS: DARTH MAUL (2000) 1
BY DREW STRUZAN

STAR WARS: DARTH MAUL (2000) 2
BY DREW STRUZAN

STAR WARS: DARTH MAUL (2000) 3
BY DREW STRUZAN

STAR WARS: DARTH MAUL (2000) 4
BY DREW STRUZAN

STAR WARS

DARTH MAUL 1

DARTH MAUL™

RON MARZ
JAN DUURSEMA
RICK MAGYAR

EXCLUSIVE

STAR WARS: DARTH MAUL (2000) 1
DYNAMIC FORCES PHOTO VARIANT

STAR WARS: DARTH MAUL (2000) 1
PHOTO VARIANT

STAR WARS®

DARTH MAUL™

STAR WARS

DARTH MAUL 2 OF 4

$2.99 US
$4.50 CAN

MARZ
DUURSEMA
MAGYAR

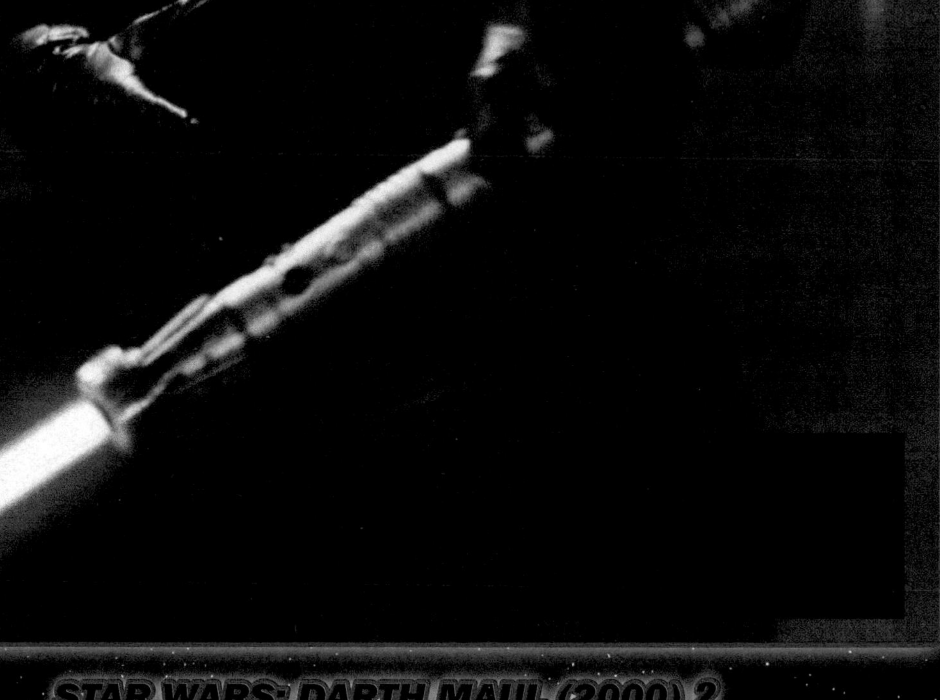

STAR WARS: DARTH MAUL (2000) 2
PHOTO VARIANT

STAR WARS®
DARTH MAUL™

DARTH
MAUL
3 OF 4

$2.99 US
$4.50 CAN

MARZ
DUURSEMA
MAGYAR

STAR WARS: DARTH MAUL (2000) 3
PHOTO VARIANT

STAR WARS

STAR WARS

DARTH MAUL

DARTH
MAUL
4 OF 4

$2.99 US
$4.50 CAN

MARZ
DUURSEMA
MAGYAR

STAR WARS: DARTH MAUL (2000) 4
PHOTO VARIANT

STAR WARS: DARTH MAUL — DEATH SENTENCE 1
BY DAVE DORMAN

STAR WARS TALES 9
BY JON FOSTERA

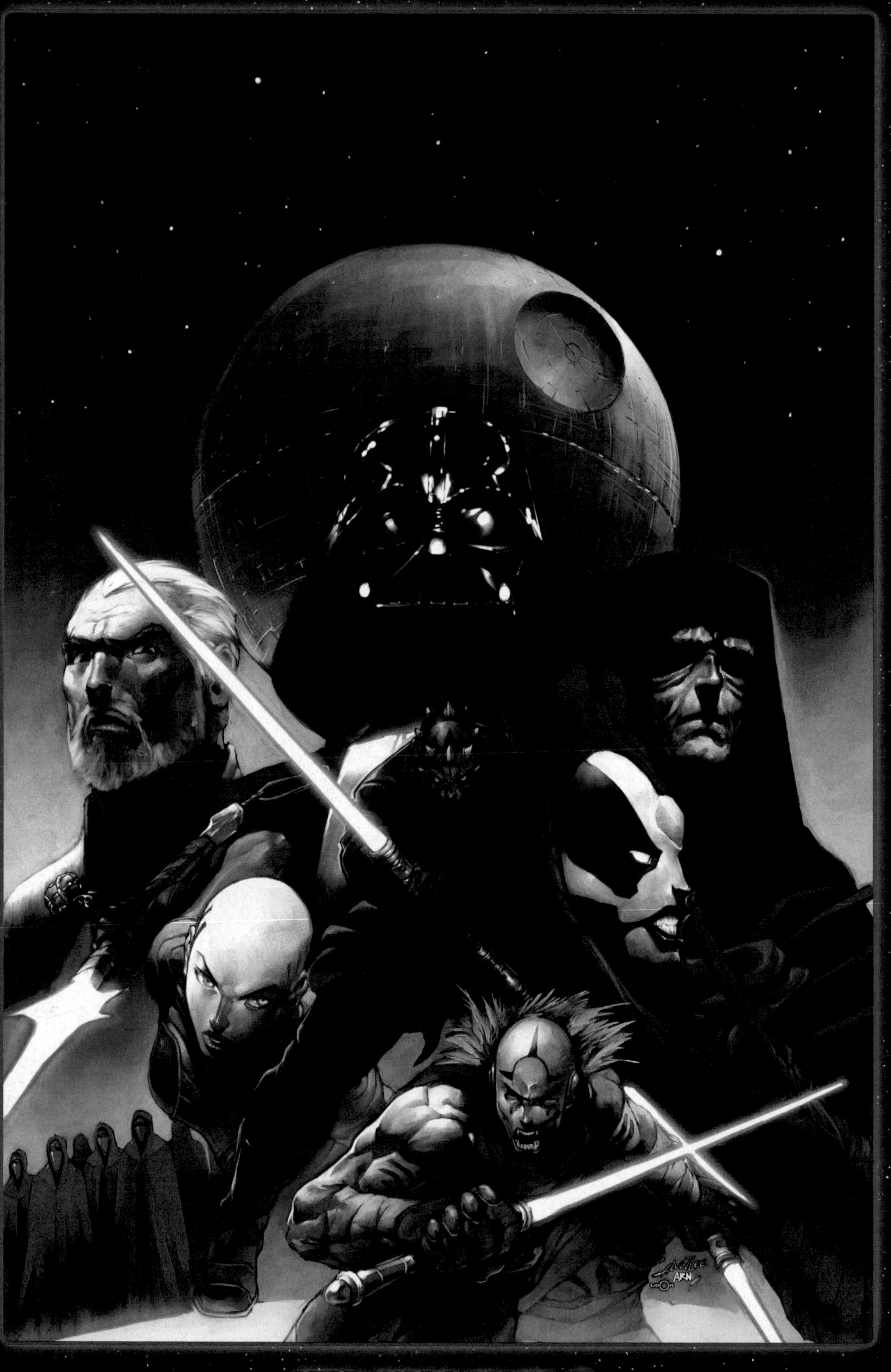

STAR WARS TALES 17
BY ALVIN LEE & UDON

STAR WARS TALES 17
PHOTO VARIANT

STAR WARS TALES 24
PHOTO VARIANT

STAR WARS TALES VOL. 5 TPB
BY TSUNEO SANDA

STAR WARS: EPISODE I - THE PHANTOM MENACE 3
BY HUGH FLEMING

STAR WARS: EPISODE I THE PHANTOM MENACE 3
PHOTO VARIANT

STAR WARS: EPISODE I THE PHANTOM MENACE 4
BY HUGH FLEMING

STAR WARS®

THE PHANTOM MENACE

This is number 370 of 750

copies of the limited edition of

STAR WARS: EPISODE I THE PHANTOM MENACE,

each of which has been individually

signed by cover illustrator

RAVENWOOD.

Ravenwood

STAR WARS: EPISODE I THE PHANTOM MENACE
LIMITED-EDITION HC TIP-IN PLATE ART
BY RAVENWOOD

STAR WARS: EPISODE I THE PHANTOM MENACE MANGA
VOL. 1-2 DIGEST
BY KIA ASAMIYA

UNUSED STAR WARS: EPISODE I THE PHANTOM MENACE
ART PUBLISHED IN THE STAR WARS ART: COMICS HARDCOVER

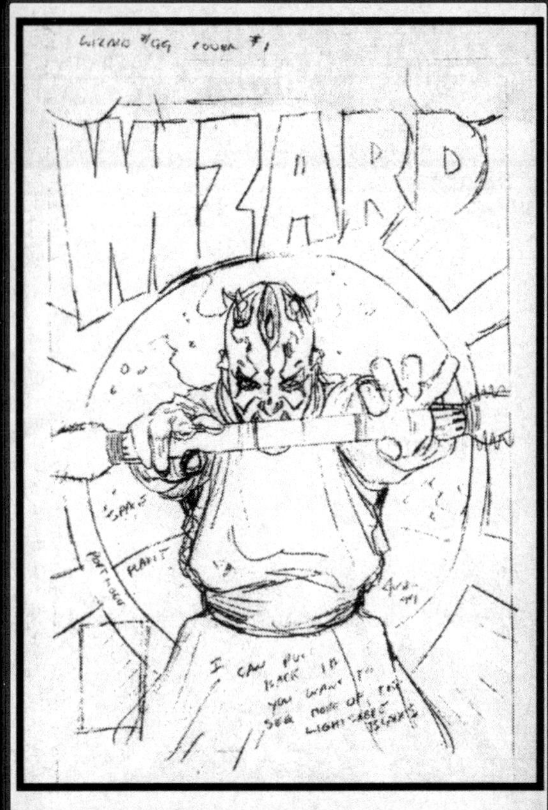

WIZARD 99
SKETCHES BY JOE JUSKO

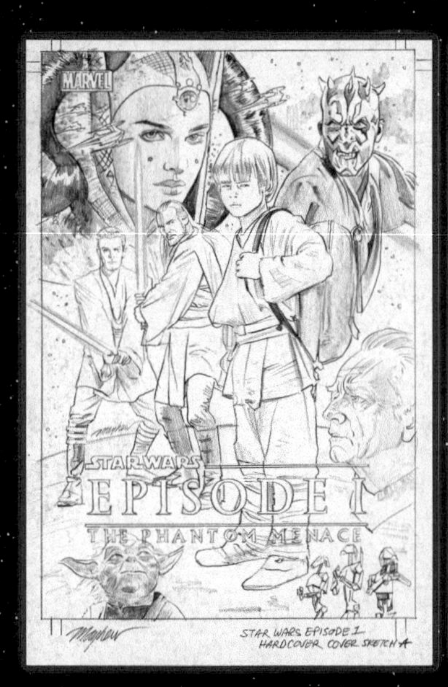

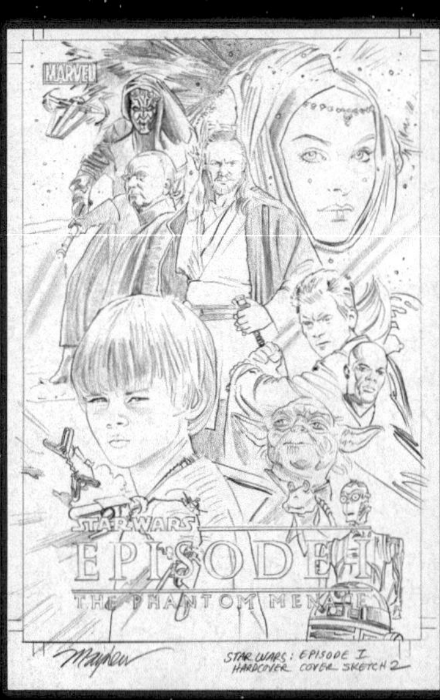

STAR WARS: EPISODE I THE PHANTOM MENACE HC
COVER PROCESS BY MIKE MAYHEW

CHECK IT OUT!

THE NEW SPIDER-MAN!

FIRST APPEARANCE! SPIDER-MAN UNLIMITED #1/2

WIZARD®

THIS ISSUE BELONGS TO DOOM!

wizardworld.com

COUNTDOWN TO WIZARD 2000

ISSUES TO GO 01

JUSKO 99

the comics magazine • 99

WIZARD 99
BY JOE JUSKO

STAR WARS: EPISODE I THE PHANTOM MENACE HC
BY MIKE MAYHEW

STAR WARS: DARTH MAUL (2000) 3
PAGES 15-18 BY JUAN FRIGERI & MAURO VARGAS

STAR WARS: DARTH MAUL (2000) 4
PAGES 10-13 BY JUAN FRIGERI & MAURO VARGAS